To my dear
You are a
for Jesus.
of God carry you to new
heights in Him.
Love
M.

MW00960893

ISBN
LCCN

Printed in the United States of America

Table of Contents

Dedication I

Acknowledgements IV

Introduction...V

Preface From a Mother VIII

Comments of a Counselor..XIII

Queen of Commerce Avenue.......................................1

Marriage and Infertility...10

Children 15

Foster Daughters: Krista and Katie...........................19

Abandonment & Grief 25

Our Family Grows 29

I Was Adopted 38

Troubled Waters 46

Mission to Mexico 62

First Search for Birth Parents 67

Mandy Parenting..73

Residual Pain 88

Mandy's Birth Mother 93

Court Intervention..96

Getting On With Life...104

A Word in Time..109

Nevertheless..116

Chad Parenting...119

Reunion in Prison 126

Grandparents Parenting 132

Big Changes..137

Jenna Has a Baby...141

Truth from Jason..146

More Birth Parents...152

Letting Go..161

The Battle Against Cancer..170

Father Knows Best..180

Facing My Own Issues 185

Update on Our Family 192

Counselors Summary...205

Addendum A: Revisiting Infertility Grief 209

Addendum B: Family Mental Health Issues........................212

Addendum C: Recommended Sources of Information..........220

References..222

Dedication

To

The Lord Jesus Christ.

You first loved me.

Thank you for trusting Terry and me to be parents.

To Terry:

My dear husband, you have been faithful to stand with our family and me all these years. Because of your willingness we now have a legacy, a family, a story, and now a book. We have made this journey, with God's grace poured on us abundantly. Thank you for loving me, and being a "father" to our children. You are a man with a Joseph anointing; just as Joseph cared for Jesus and Mary, you have cared for our family, providing marvelous stability and humor along the way.

To Jason:

Our first son, who I loved from the moment I laid eyes on you in the social worker's office, on that cold winter morning in 1969. Your blue eyes, blond hair, and infectious smile captured my heart. It has been my joy to be your mom, to grow with you, to cry with you, to play with you and to be good friends today. I love you even though you beat me at Scrabble.

I

To Mandy:

You are our darling first daughter, the second child to come to our family. My first sight of you with your round face, bald head and quick smile gave me joy from the moment I saw you in the swinging cradle. You are my daughter. Forgive me for my unconsciously wanting you to be who I wanted you to be. You are uniquely special and I am learning to accept your specialness. I love you and am so grateful you are alive. You love to laugh and tease. I love how you say "OHHH" in the cutest sweetest way when you are touched by what is said. You have challenged me to grow and taught me so much about love. I will always love you.

To Chad:

You, our second son, are Korean, adorable, shy, dark skinned, tentative, and kind. Because you so delighted us, we decided to have more children from Korea. I love you. You are gifted, intelligent, patient, and humorous. You were so easy to raise, maybe too much so, as you, the middle child, deserved so much more attention. I enjoy and savor every new thing I learn about you for I want to know you more. It is my hope that someday we will be able to sit and talk openly, totally accepting one another.

To Jenna:

You, our second daughter, our fourth child, you also came from Korea. How I love you. You moved fast from the moment you came home to us, and you still do today. You are my high-energy bundle of ideas, plans, and places to go. You were adorable as a baby, a teen, and are a beauty today. I am grateful for our relationship today, as two women, who love God and each other. Your gifts of humor, rapid speech, and endless energy are a part of the woman I love so much!

To Todd:

You, our third son, our fifth child, came to us from Korea after a five-year wait. You are the last but never the least of my children. You were Mr. Friendly from the first week you came home, charming folks at the grocery store with your big "hi!" and smile. I love how verbal you are especially when you share your thoughts and dreams with me. You have a tender heart, humility and a willingness to ask forgiveness. You love visiting with people and finding out the "details" of their lives. You are generous and full of mercy. I find satisfaction in that you enjoy learning about my life as a child growing up and the events of my life now.

To Krista and Katie:

Our two wonderful foster daughters. God had a huge plan to bless our entire family and especially me by adding two lovely teens to our family forty years ago. You both have given back to us 100 fold blessings compared with the short time we provided you a home. You have given us your love, forgiveness, friendship and prayers over the years. You have given us six amazing grandchildren. I love you both, so much, and thank God for allowing us to be family now and for eternity.

Acknowledgements

A special thanks to my three diligent editors, Sonja Kvale, Terry Jones, Karen Schoewe, and Jenny Mechtel. Thank you for your tireless efforts. You four made this project possible.

Introduction

At various times while raising our family, Terry and I have both felt hurled down a river of circumstances with currents we never wanted to swim in, yet by God's grace we not only survived, we thrived. Our life has had some very hard times but it has also been very fulfilling. We are here today enjoying life and thanking God.

> "Many waters cannot quench love; rivers cannot sweep it away." Song of Solomon 8:7

God's love is more than I can comprehend. It is His very nature. Terry and I have faced many challenges parenting our five adopted children. Without God's love for us, neither our marriage, nor either of us would have survived. The troubled waters we navigated would have washed over us, and we would have drowned. We are here today as a family, loving and doing life together.

This book is my memoir of our journey, of God's helping me to love and grow in the midst of many circumstances beyond my control. As each of my family read the book, and reported back to me, I realized that their memories sometimes varied from mine. I attempted to convey my "heart" feelings as these different events unfolded. Each adult read the manuscript and gave me their input on their memory of things. These discussions proved healing for each of us I believe, and were a bonus from writing the book.

I chose the book title, "Many Waters Cannot Quench Love" to say that all the trials and struggles and fires we went through as a family has not diminished my love for any of my children. Some of the choices our children have made have taken us places we never wanted to go and exposed us to situations we would never have chosen. Through all the circumstances of our family's journey God's grace has been there for us. Our love for each child has not diminished; rather it has matured and deepened. God's grace has kept us from drowning in floods of turbulent times. His grace is enough. Our love for one another has survived them, even in all our unlovable times. The following story tells you how it happened.

My children will always have my love no matter what they do. I feel like I understand in some small way, the boundless immeasurable love our Father God pours on us. His love is extravagant, free, and waiting!

There is enough love for each child. Love for one doesn't deplete the amount I can give to another. Each child holds a unique place in my heart, which no one else can fill or satisfy.

Comments in Italics throughout the book are those of Dr. Sonja Kvale, LPC. To learn more about Dr. Kvale's work, visit the website www.mirrorimagesretreats.org:

This is Josie's story, not only of the events of the turbulent river ride through her life and the lives of her adopted children but it also includes her struggles to find the significant life rafts to help her survive. This search for understanding herself and her children has strengthened her. God has helped to sustain her during the falls and rapids of life, maintaining her in a place of peace and security.

It is her prayer and mine that these words may help encourage parents, particularly those of adoptive children, and the children who have been adopted, to come to a secure, steady place in their journeys. It is our desire that they may know and recognize they are loved by others and by their creator God. May this love help them embrace their own journeys.

Webster's first definition of family is: all the people living in the same house. Whether people are blood related or adopted or under foster care these individuals are family. The interrelated aspect of co-habitation is what makes individuals a family. The sharing of life experience is one of the strongest bonding agents throughout a lifetime but it does not always occur. Bonding of family members is not guaranteed whether biological or adopted.

One person is not a family. Family occurs as people share their time and space with one another. The trials of life, each individual's struggles, affect each individual within the family, because they are brought together to share time and space with each other. John Donne wrote a poem titled "No man is an island." This indicates that we are all interrelated, one with another. Because we are family we have an effect on one another.

Can we walk away? Yes. Can we overprotect or control? Yes, and everything in between is possible too. One of life's truths is that we are all interconnected with one another. We can learn how to communicate and relate effectively to those around us, within the family and outside the family.

Preface From a Mother

I would be a rich woman if I had a dollar for every person who has told me, "You should write a book about what has happened in your family!" After hearing this enough times, I began to believe I did have something valuable to share. My story is about parenting but particularly for adoptive parents, adoptees and *all* those whose lives have been touched by adoption. It is a thrill for me that I am now able to chronicle a forty-year journey of adoption. From the time we started thinking about our family until today we have adopted five children, welcomed two foster daughters, and parented two of our nineteen grandchildren. We have met birth parents; we have even experienced the burial of a birth parent. This is a picture of the journey through three generations of our family.

I write from a Christian perspective. Many other books cover the psychological, cultural, and sociological aspects. I believe adoption has a spiritual dynamic that is often overlooked. My belief is that the trauma of separation at birth causes spiritual and emotional wounding to a child, which can only be healed through acknowledging the loss, grieving it, and receiving spiritual restoration.

This book is not a *study* about adoption; it is a story of *a real family*; a story of a Christian mom's real life journey through the process of parenting from birth to adulthood. It is a story of our struggles to graft into our family, our five adopted children. I believe that many of our experiences as a family will help some readers cope in their own personal journey. I hope the candor with which I share events will prove healing to those who need it.

My hesitation in publishing was that I don't have a storybook ending to our journey. One friend commented to me that this was good, because many people write their success stories, but few things are written about how to be victorious in the trenches with our daily walk with the Lord. Jesus Christ has been and continues to be the source of my strength and joy each day of this journey.

Some will find our story discouraging. Others may find hope for their lives; even rejoice in their journey, thanking God for the grace they have experienced. I used the Bible as God's instruction manual to help me live by His plan for my life. I was often lost or overwhelmed and turned to the Word of God. You will find me quoting scripture throughout my story because it helped so much on my journey. My intent is to give encouragement, hope, healing, understanding, and empathy to others who are or have been touched by the struggles of adoption. Early in our adoption experience a social worker spoke to a group of us adoptive parents at Family Services in our town. She said we each needed to accept the fact that our adopted child was a "special needs child" by nature of the adoption. I didn't receive this very well. In fact, I got angry, thinking that she didn't know *my* children. They were generally "fine", and she did them a disservice by that statement. Today, I agree with her one hundred percent.

Adopted children have special needs in the sense that their spirit was wounded at the time of separation from their birth parents. I believe that until this grief is addressed, adoptees are influenced and controlled by the trauma in more ways than they understand. Facing the loss can help adoptees more fully embrace life and understand their own choices and emotions.

As I have learned to relax and trust God with my children's lives, He set me free to enjoy them and life more. Before trusting God I was trying to control relationships and force bonding, which can only be done cooperatively by people who choose to be in relationship. We have closeness with some of our family and for this we are ever grateful. With some, we have given up our own expectations of connectedness, accepting the reality that each individual determines their own depth of involvement in relationships. We pray God's blessing into all their lives and stay open to the depth of relationship and trust they are willing to share with us.

Adoption is God's idea. Pharaoh's daughter adopted Moses, the great leader of Israel. Joseph adopted Jesus Himself, not being of his natural bloodline. Adoption is a complicated process that tugs at the heartstrings in ways I don't think any of the triad could have possibly comprehended. The triad consists of the birth parents, adoptive parents and adoptive child/adult. Each member of the triad must find their way to love and accept each other, for their life to be lived to its fullest measure. Just as God never forces Himself on us but lets us choose Him, we as adoptive parents and adopted adults must choose to love one another.

I hope my writing gives insight and a fresh perspective on a delicate matter of the heart. May you honor and treasure our journey for what it is and is not.

To respect the privacy of all involved, all the names and places have been changed. All the events are true and really happened. I tell my stories from my own understanding and perspective knowing that the memories of those involved may not be the same as mine. The family members have previewed their portion of the manuscript.

This book is a history of God's grace poured out on the Jones family. His grace covered our marriage, our adoptions of five children, our two foster daughters and parenting two grandchildren. This book is a memoir of my life as an adoptive mom. The writing has helped me clarify my feelings and understand and accept the multiple relationships involved in our family. I had great fear in undertaking this project. I didn't want to relive the painful memories. It felt like "undressing" as I opened my heart, deepest thoughts and emotions to others.

We celebrated our fortieth wedding anniversary with a three-day weekend with all our children and grandchildren. The blessing and reality is that we are all in fact, functioning, loving each other, and attempting to accept one another. We have had some very rough water, but God has helped me to be grateful for our family, for what is going well, and for the uniqueness of each individual person.

Part of me wanted to write the book to let other struggling parents know they are not alone in their efforts to create a loving, healthy family environment for their adopted children. We had many struggles, and I know from talking to other adoptive parents we are not alone. Our journey is unique to us, because of Terry and my family dynamics in our families of origin; and because of the distinct cultural, spiritual, and genetic background each of our children brought to our family. If in reading this book, you get one thought, suggestion, or helpful idea on how to cope with your adoptive relationship, I will consider my writing to have value.

My hope is that our story will give you encouragement and courage to continue your journey. I hope you will consider turning to God, His grace and His Word to navigate the often-turbulent waters of parenting. I have found the following verses to be a foundation for me, when all around me life seemed to be falling apart.

> "God is our refuge and strength, an ever present help in trouble." Psalm 46:1
>
> "The name of the Lord is a fortified tower, the righteous run to it and are safe." Proverbs 18:10

God can and will help you through any situation. He is waiting to be invited in. During our entire journey I never felt abandoned by God; He always gave me some sign to show me He was working on our family's behalf. 2 Chronicles 16:9 says "The eyes of the Lord range throughout the whole earth to strengthen those whose hearts are fully committed to Him."

There were more good times in our years of parenting than bad ones. God always showed up and helped us with a way through the troubles. We're here today happy, growing and learning, all because of God's faithfulness.

As you read on, it is my prayer that Father God's love and hope shine through to you. Moses, Esther, Samuel, and even Jesus had at least one adoptive parent. They all had specific callings on their lives. I believe each child has a specific purpose and calling in life. I believe God specifically picked our children for us, knowing who we were, what we needed to learn, and how we would relate to these particular children. God has a plan, and we are privileged to partake in it but we do not know what lies ahead.

Comments of a Counselor

When a sperm and an egg join together within the uterus to begin a new life it is a very special gift from the Creator God. Conception is not a chance occurrence. Every new life presents a need for change and adjustment for all involved. Many changes must be faced. Each pregnancy creates challenges for the mother, the father, and the siblings. All the family members must face changes in their space and relationships. A new baby in the family creates a change, or crisis, in every family, every time. Even the baby must grow and develop, changing enough to survive life independently outside the womb.

In today's world there are options for those unwilling to face the consequences of parenting this new forming life. These are abortion and adoption, both legal; however, both of these options have eternal consequences.

*Abortion by the birth parents is the ultimate form of abuse and destroys life. In our present culture, abortion has become a legal option for those **unwilling** to face the changes necessary to incorporate a new life into their life space. Those who are unwilling to become a parent to the life beginning within the mother's body can legally dispose of that child. There are consequences to this choice. The baby's life is destroyed and those responsible for the choice of destruction are accountable for this choice and must face the consequences that may be physical, emotional, sexual and/or spiritual.*

Adoption gives the baby a chance for continued life initiated at conception. Adoption has become a viable option for those who consider themselves unable or unwilling to become parents yet are willing to accept the gift of this new life given to them. The choice of adoption means that parent/parents pass on the responsibility and the privilege of caring for this life to other humans. The adoptive parents are those who "choose" to accept the privilege of caring for these children as well as the lifelong responsibilities of parenting. The birth parents that choose giving away the child will have to ultimately face the realization their child is living and growing older somewhere beyond them.

The major consequence of adoption for the infant is a sense of abandonment by the birth mother. Abandonment is the ultimate form of neglect. Neglect has consequences for an individual because there is no event seen as evidence for the sense of worthlessness.

Babies within the womb react physically to sounds before birth. The sense of hearing is present before birth. The newborn infant recognizes the voices of the parents and this is evident in that there is a calming effect on a newborn when held by the mother. The mother's heart beat sounds and rhythm has been a part of the baby's life since its conception. A baby can be calmed sooner when held close to the mother's heart beat rather than when held by another person. This separation from the mother at birth has a profound effect on the infant when those voices and sounds are no longer a part of life. An infant cannot express this, but the loss is more than likely the underlying frustration that an adopted child has to deal with and come to understand as a part of who they are, and why they are whom they are. This break from the known may occur twice or more times if an infant is placed in foster care before the adoptive family gets custody. An infant has no words or explanation available to express their fear and anxiety at this time in their lives.

A child's understanding is not the final truth and must be addressed when older and wiser in order to reinterpret, grasp and deal with the whole truth of who they are. The combination of the early abandonment does impact the person, but also the in-grafting into a new family has an equally important impact on each life. We are not, any one of us, separate beings. Each of us is a sum total of our life experiences and relationships. Until we integrate these we can feel fragmented. Consideration of the whole of one's own life's experience combined with the reality of the experience of the other peoples' reality helps to heal and restore each of us to a place of peace.

The search for the whole truth is a healthy adventure for each of us. Those courageous enough will dare to look at their childhood perceptions. An adult can retrieve the truth by review and re-interpretation together with the additional input of others' realities and come to know the whole truth. Knowing that there has been a plan by a Creator God for each life and it is ultimately for the good of each person gives us the courage to look and discover how all of life works together.

There is the age old debate in child development of which factor is most influential in a person's life. Is it the environment within which one is raised that is the most important factor? Or is it heredity? This has also become known with newer terms as "nature vs. nurture." Although understanding the effects of both, I also do not have the answer to the question of which of these two is most important in a person's development.

1

Queen of Commerce Avenue

Standing on the hill of the convent compound, I watched the dancing lights of the city below me. I felt torn between the two worlds; I wanted to serve God but cloistered living was such a sobering experience for me. The allure of the city and life in the world pulled at me. I stood there crying that lonely night, asking God to show me how to be successful and happy as a nun. I wanted a husband. I wanted babies! As I looked at the city lights I fought with the reality that I wanted to be out under the city lights, a part of the world.

I thought about who I was and pondered how I had gotten there in the first place.

I was Josie, fourth child of John and Sarah Becker, sandwiched in the middle, fourth of eight children. Tragically my mom frequently laughed and said, "I only wanted one child." That statement had sunk deep into my spirit, and I grew up feeling unworthy, guilty, and sad, thinking I was a burden for my mother. My thinking is an example of how a child understands and establishes words as truth. This became a "fact" for me. I lived with a sense of guilt for being a burden, and did all I could to take care of myself, to ease my mother's burden.

I determined early in life that I would "carry my own weight". We called it "fend for yourself" as I was growing up. I played this role out by taking responsibility for myself, to earn all my own money, paying for my own clothes, and all my own expenses. It was NOT something my parents had asked of me or expected; it was an inner vow I made.

Ours was a typical Catholic family of the 1940-70's. Birth control was considered a serious sin; so many couples had large families. Personally, I was very glad to be alive! My childhood was spent as a tomboy, climbing trees, playing basketball with the neighbor kids, and building "chugs" (motor-less go-carts) in the alley with my big brother Will. There were three families that hung out together, ours with eight children, the Smith family with six children, and the Woski family with just two children. The Woski's daughter was Sandi, "The Queen!" Sandi was tall, thin, self-assured with pretty green eyes.

My dad was very religious, so we attended church and mass frequently. My parents never entertained the idea that we would go to the "wicked" public school. We were Catholic through and through, and parochial school was our only option. My older brother Will purposely misbehaved to get expelled from our school, so he could go with his buddies to *public* school. It was shameful to my parents and me when this happened.

My parents fought constantly. They never seemed to even like each other. There was always tension in our home, adding to the obvious chaos of daily life with eight children. The other pressure I felt was from sharing my bedroom with a younger sister Tess, who had mental health issues. These were undiagnosed at that time, so my parents fumbled along trying to keep my sister in school. By fifth grade she entered a school for mentally challenged children. This was a huge stigma. Tess suffered from rejection most of her life.

Our family time usually took place on Sundays. Mom would pack a picnic lunch Sunday afternoon and we would drive into the country together. Mom packed a nice hot meal, not just sandwiches, and off we'd go, about 4 pm on Sunday. It usually took mom that long to get things together, with my dad fussing at her to get going. He never offered any help to mom with these household chores. (I am embarrassed to admit I never offered much help to get these meals

2

ready, even at age sixteen or seventeen, thinking that's what moms do!) We kids loved these adventures. We climbed rocks, went swimming, and hiked in the woods.

Dad often took us to the beach on lazy summer days. He worked the afternoon shift at the newspaper, so we had until 3 pm to enjoy the lake. Dad would pile the entire neighborhood gang into the car and off we'd go to the beach for the afternoon. This was long before seatbelts so we could crowd ten to twelve kids into the car. He would read his paper, or sleep while we swam. We would play in the water and when he was ready to leave we would beg, "Can we stay just five more minutes?" I always felt loved by my dad because he always wanted us with him. He never left the house without inviting us, "Does anyone want to come along?" I always wanted to go along because I got one-on-one time with Dad. I was a willing "goer" from an early age. I loved to be with Dad, meeting new people, and seeing new places.

My mom stayed home and did all the household chores. I enjoyed helping do the laundry because that gave me a chance to visit with Mom. I would use a stick to pass the very hot clothes through the old fashioned washing machine. I pushed the clothes through the old wringer on their way to the rinse tubs. Mom would then swing the wringer and again feed the clothes into the second tub. There were lots of clothes, for lots of kids. We spent many hours together on laundry day. Mom was cheerful, often times whistling a lovely tune as she worked. One time mom confided that she whistled when she was upset, as a way to relieve her stress. I always wished I hadn't known that, because it was nicer to assume her whistling was a happy sound.

Mom slept late every day, usually until one PM. Most summer days she stayed in her pajamas, saying it was too hot to get dressed. This was before the days of air conditioning. Mom sat at our kitchen table smoking cigarettes for several hours, drinking coffee and visiting with whoever would come her way. Mom's burst of energy usually began about ten thirty at night.

It wasn't until I was in seventh grade and went to visit other families that I began to realize our family was different. Other moms got dressed every day and even left their homes. These moms did the grocery shopping, and even had lady friends into their homes. I never could get either of my parents to come to any of my school events. I'd ask them to come to watch me as a cheerleader or softball player, but the answer was always the same: they were either too busy, or too tired. I felt I was unimportant to them.

From the age of twelve years on I felt some responsibility for Tess, my younger sister, worrying about her safety. My parents totally disagreed on how to discipline Tess or whether or not they should discipline her, so the tension kept mounting between them. My mom would refuse to talk to my dad for months on end. I was the self-appointed mediator, trying to get everyone to forgive and get along. (Of course hindsight is always clearer, and I now realize that my mom herself was traumatized by my sister's behavior, and had no help coping with her. I guess maybe she thought there wasn't any help, or was too proud to ask for help.)

Tess was an adorable blonde, three years younger than me. Both Tess and my next brother Tim struggled with school. Tess was always the brunt of teasing on the way to school. My father was very strict, harsh and demeaning in his attempts to help them with their schoolwork. I got praise from my dad for my good grades but then I would feel guilty for being smart. I actually enjoyed learning. I had to watch my siblings at the dining room table being relentlessly and harshly corrected, shamed until they would begin crying over their inability to comprehend either the math or the spelling.

When I would go to my mom with disagreements and problems between Tess and I, Mom always chided me as the older sister,

"You're mature, you handle it." What I heard was that my feelings didn't matter. The truth was I had no idea how to handle the situations, but I was asking for the support of my parents to cope with the pain of having disabled siblings. I felt responsible but had no authority to take action. This always ended in my frustration. One time I found an empty closet in the attic and put a lock on it, to keep Tess from stealing my clothes. I had purchased these clothes with my own money. She wore them, soiled them, and then stuffed them under our mattress. My mom was furious, saying I was overreacting, and made me take the lock off the closet. The stealing continued. I was told to handle the situation, but when I did I was reprimanded. It seemed as if it was a lose-lose situation.

As I reflect back on life, this is why I became idealistic, and expected so much of myself, since I was always told to handle it myself. To this day whenever anyone is involved in stealing and lying, it triggers such fear, rage, and anxiety in me. This was particularly true when it involved our children, I felt like I was living with my sister again. I have had to learn to reason through these feelings and choose not to let these feelings overwhelm me. I am more able to reason my way through to another response.

I was a homecoming queen candidate in high school and I was so worried my parents wouldn't come to the crowning, like the other parents. Mom always seemed preoccupied with daily life, and didn't want to participate in what was happening outside the home. To my delight they came for the Homecoming game and the crowning at half time.

After high school graduation I entered the convent. I had been in parochial education for twelve years. Sister Andrea, my science and photography teacher had been a great mentor to me all through high school. I served on the yearbook and newspaper staff, so that meant spending lots of time in the dark room developing pictures, with her leaning over my shoulder, teaching and directing me. I loved my one on one talks with her. She actually listened to me and cared about my life. It was therefore a logical goal for me to want to become a nun like her. I loved God with all my heart, as long as I can remember. Going into this convent, a teaching order of nuns, seemed like a good plan for my life. There were, however, three problems with this choice: I liked boys, I didn't want to be a teacher, and I *really* wanted to be a mom. But I followed after the person who had nurtured me, in conflict with my own desires.

My dad had studied to be a priest. My parents were tickled pink that one of their kids wanted to have "a vocation," as it was called in those days. My parents held clergy in high esteem. So off to the convent I went on a lovely fall day, with very mixed emotions, excited to be doing God's will, pleasing my parents yet afraid if I did not go I would be displeasing God.

The first step of entering the convent was to be a postulant. Our class was a group of eager and enthusiastic young women. We started out with forty-two energetic young women, ready to take on the challenge of college studies and communal living for the next year, preparing to be nuns. By Christmas we were down to about thirty of us.

I realized I was not doing well with convent life. I loved my classmates, my studies, and the environment; but, then I would chide myself for not being willing to "take up my cross and follow Christ." Even as I write I can see more clearly God's plan for me was being brought out on that hill at night. God had planted the desire within me to be living in the world, not within a cloister. (He knew I would travel to many nations with the gospel, in the future.)

In the late evening hours I would go knock on Mother Superior's door, much like Maria VonTrapp in *The Sound of Music*, and spend hours talking with her. I had questions about what to expect as a nun, and how I would cope with the next year of cloistering, with no outside contact at all.

Finally, one night in March, after six months of my tears and talking, Mother Superior said, "Josie, I don't think this is for you. God wants us happy and you don't seem very happy here."

I looked at her and said, "So you think God would still love me even if I don't become a nun?"

"Absolutely. Call your parents and go home."

So at 2 a.m., with my leader's blessing, I called home. Dad answered; he was very surprised but very supportive of my decision. I asked if he approved. Dad said, "Absolutely, come home." So at seven a.m. the next day I took off my nun's uniform (the habit), put on my regular street clothes, and met my parents at a side entrance of the convent. I wasn't allowed to tell anyone I was leaving, for fear of endangering their vocational calling! How ridiculous, now as I look back, that the staff feared my leaving would jeopardize someone else's calling. Surely God was big enough to guard the hearts of those He had called. My roommate left the convent a year after me. We were attendants in each other's weddings and are still good friends. Today Jan and I have many fond memories of early morning prayers (vespers) in the lovely chapel, homemade bread with honey for afternoon snacks, and trying to "outdo" each other with our good deeds in the convent, competing to accumulate the most points for heaven.

I came home from the convent, got a job at a medical clinic and enrolled in college choosing social work as a career path. I had a boyfriend when I left for the convent. When I returned home I had one date with him. He and his friends were involved in drinking parties; so one date was enough for me to know I wasn't interested in him anymore. I wanted more than *that* for my life.

7

I decided to go on with my education at a prestigious Catholic girl's college. Shortly thereafter my girlfriend lined me up with a blind date with Terry! He had gone to my high school and remembered me! He called me and asked me right off the top, "Josie, what are you doing out of the convent?"

We went dancing on our first date and the romance began.

On the second date, when Terry came to pick me up, my house was on fire! What was happening? The second mattress fire occurring in our home in two weeks! We left the house and went dancing again! While we were on the dance floor we talked about the trauma of the fire and my tears flowed while Terry comforted me. His mercy melted my heart.

Tess set fire to our home on three different occasions when she was sixteen and I was nineteen years old. My oldest brother's bed was ignited first, and then the next brother's bed and the third fire was my parent's bed. By the third time, the fire department and our family were sure it wasn't an accident. Tess admitted she had started the fires and the county welfare department sent her to a detention home for nine months. After this she spent time at the mental health ward of the hospital. (Tess was fifty-five years old before I discovered the reason she had done this. She had been molested by two of our brothers whose mattresses she burned. She was totally traumatized and was responding out of fear and rage in her heart. Tess had told our mom about the abuse but Mom refused to believe her. The third mattress burned was Mom and Dad's.)

Terry was by my side and walked with me through this chaos. We went to Terry's brother's wedding about two months later and by then I thought… "I could marry this guy!"

Terry and I dated three years while the turmoil continued within my family. I wanted to get out of my parents' home, but my money had to go for school expenses, not living expenses. This was a hard decision but it was a good one for me. I needed and wanted an education.

Terry teased me by calling me "The Queen of Commerce Avenue" as a little inside joke. This was his way of flattering me. We knew another girl, who also lived on Commerce Avenue, who was very popular at our high school, and kids called her "The Queen of Commerce Avenue," but Terry would always tease me and say, "Not to worry! You are the *real* queen!" I loved Terry's affirmations, his acceptance, humor and love for me. These were all reasons I was attracted to him as a partner.

2

Marriage and Infertility

Since we had no money, our dates had to be creative. In the fall and winter before we married, Terry and I would often take long walks, strolling in neighborhoods past stately older homes. The smell of wood burning in fireplaces wafting through the air invited us into an imaginary family world. A mom and a dad sitting around the fire, reading stories to pajama clad children snuggled on their parents' laps. We dreamed about owning a home with a fireplace someday. We'd talk nonstop planning our married life. We would have six children, since we both came from large families and loved kids, and felt confident in relating to them. I felt prepared to be a parent because I babysat from the time I was ten until I was twenty-one years old. I loved the children I watched and the money I was able to earn for college. I worked for several large Catholic families who I felt very close to and they had become my role models of a Godly family life for me.

During our dating years, my sister Tess married and became pregnant right away. Two months after our marriage, my sister Tess's six month old daughter died. It was a SIDS death (Sudden Infantile Death Syndrome). There were family rumors that Tess's husband had been involved in the death but no one followed up to prove or disprove any connection. Tess and her husband divorced after the baby's death, and my sense of responsibility for Tess increased. I worried deeply about her safety.

Terry and I wanted time for each other so we decided we would wait for a year before we would have children. The "marvelous" world of contraception was upon us so we could control things, or so we thought, even when our religion preached against such things. We soon found out we could not control everything.

We were practicing Catholics and attended a married couples retreat each year. It was a cold February weekend as we entered the Franciscan retreat center, for our annual "marital checkup." We looked at these times as necessary to be with each other and God. The first evening we were there less than two hours when the priest in charge called us to his office for a talk. He wanted to know why there were no children yet, after two years of marriage. How times have changed. No one would ever ask that of someone today. My first boss, during the interview process for my job as a county social worker, asked what guarantee he could have that I wouldn't get pregnant in the first year of work. He asked for a verbal commitment from me to work for a year before starting our family before he would hire me. I agreed.

After the first year, we put aside the contraceptives and began anticipating pregnancy. No pregnancy resulted. We went from our place of controlling conception to a place of inability to conceive. We had not been in control. Was God punishing us? What was happening? We wanted children. We wanted six children! Our plan was not happening. What was wrong?

We felt we'd done everything we knew to do to conceive except stand me on my head after intercourse! We knew of a couple that had been advised to try this so the sperm would go down into the uterus and they had been successful. We began using fertility drugs to increase our ability to conceive a child. We tried artificial insemination with Terry's sperm. We would rush the bottle off to the Doctor's office, hoping no one knew we had just "had sex". We tried the insemination procedure three times. After the third attempt I was driving to work, only to be interrupted by pains so severe I had to stop the car and sit on the curb. A gentleman saw me sitting there and came over to see if I needed help. This was in the days before cell phones. I asked him to call my mother-in-law to come rescue me. My mom had never learned to drive. Mom Jones took me to her home and tucked me into bed. I called the Doctor for advice.

He said, "Oops I must have injected too much fluid and sent your uterus into contractions! Just spend the day in bed and they will eventually stop!" The casualness of his reply did not endear him to me!

After a year of trying to get pregnant without success I sat in Terry's lap sobbing. All our efforts at fertility testing produced no known reason as to why we couldn't conceive. Dr. Goldsmith, the best in the fertility field at the time, had told us to go home and "relax". This was easier said than done, as I wanted so desperately to be pregnant. I shed tears of deep disappointment as Terry held me close. He kept reassuring me that this wasn't the end of the world, that we would have a family. We would adopt. I knew Terry meant what he had said and I could count on him to stick to this decision, because he was a man of his word.

After facing the reality of not being able to conceive, Terry and I agreed on adoption, so I called Family Services to set up an appointment. They invited us to an informational meeting. We went with much timidity, feeling alone in our situation. To our great surprise there were about twenty-five couples there, all inquiring about the adoption process. The social worker was very reassuring, telling us all we would be parents, and not to worry or fret about the screening process. This was before Roe vs. Wade and the carnage of abortion. Many babies were available for adoption. The social worker reassured us the home study was done so that they could match us with a child of similar background, rather than to screen us for our flaws. My family of origin had lots of problems such as alcoholism, mental illness, and trouble with the law. I was afraid they would reject us because of these things. Again the social worker assured us we would become parents sooner or later.

The information meeting was followed by many interviews. We answered many questions on how we would discipline, how we would comfort, what our weaknesses and strengths were, and how we handled differences within our marriage. They checked our bank accounts, our credit, our references, and our employers. We sometimes felt like criminals, being "investigated" for the flaws. We were glad they kept reiterating it was *not* their intent to eliminate us!

Our adoption worker Eve Font asked us many questions. One question in particular I remember was, "What do you do *for culture?*"

Terry and I looked at each other, and froze. I told her, "We like live theater productions. My dad used to take us to the science museum to see travelogues…does that count?"

On our way home Terry and I laughed about the culture question. We were both from hard working blue-collar families. Our parents watching wrestling on Friday nights probably did not qualify us as "cultured people." Our answer must have met the criteria because in two months' time we were approved to go into the "pool" of family profiles presented to the team of social workers every Monday morning. They had a committee whose job it was to match waiting children with families in the pool of waiting parents. I sure hope they prayed as they did this very important task, making decisions affecting people's lives permanently.

The word "infertile" is one no man or woman wants to hear or deal with. How does one accept this diagnosis? For a couple that planned on having six children, it was crushing news. Yet, we faltered only momentarily. As I said earlier, we cried, and then decided to investigate the idea of building our family through adoption. Our infertility had more of an impact as the years went by, but at this point we were denying the depth of our grief, and went quickly on to the adoption process seeking the children we so desperately wanted.

I had learned from trying to help Tess that mental illness could be hereditary. I was very afraid this disease would be passed down genetically, and was afraid my own children would suffer from it. Adoption felt like the perfect solution.

3

Children

Each Monday the social worker would call me and tell me about the children that were *not* chosen for us. At one of the calls she told us we almost got twins. It was emotionally draining to get these calls; always waiting for the day the group of social workers would decide we *were* the right match for a child. We told them we thought we might like a girl first.

Finally, on a crisp winter morning she called, "We have a darling little boy. Will you consider him, instead of a girl?"

We were ecstatic, "Of course!"

We came to the agency office with film, formula, diapers, and a deep joy in our hearts. Four months from our first informational and application meeting with Family Services our beautiful son Jason entered our family. The escort came bustling in holding a bundle all wrapped in receiving blankets. I pulled back the blanket to see an adorable blue eyed, fair-haired, pacifier-sucking baby, grinning at us. From the moment I laid eyes on Jason I loved him. We pulled out the plug and he laughed. Terry and I laughed with him. We could have burst we were so happy. Jason was absolutely beautiful to us. We raced home to his newly decorated bright yellow nursery with one wall of brown teddy bear wallpaper. The phone calls began. Everyone was so eager to meet our new family member. Jason settled in very easily, appearing calm and contented. We were grateful for the obvious good care he had received in the foster home. The note that accompanied him from the foster mom showed a lot of love and care. That family had called him Chris because his birth was at Christmas time.

During the application process the agency worker had mentioned that the person who would perhaps have the most trouble with the adoption would be the adoptive father's mother. True to this observation, after Terry's parents came to meet their new grandson, Terry's mom turned to us and said, "We hope the next time we come it's for your *own* baby".

I replied, "Jason is our own!"

That was the first of many hurtful remarks people would make to us over the years about our adoptive family. To be fair to Mom Jones, she was a wonderful grandma to all of our children. Mom had friends in another state, which had adopted, and were really struggling with their teenaged kids. We realized her words were more from a mother's heart of protection. I now realize I was easily offended and a lot more sensitive about infertility and adoption than I had acknowledged at that time.

Jason slept through the nights, and settled in beautifully, with no outward appearance of adjustment problems. The day he was baptized we had invited a house full of family and friends to our home for the celebration. Jason had only been in our home one week. He was still adjusting to us. We were enthusiastic about sharing him and oblivious about any confusion it may have caused him. Both of our families are large! Jason cried through the whole ceremony at church, he cried most of the day. This was Jason's most fitful day since he entered our family. I was a bit stressed...but Terry and the grandparents were around to help. Terry's mom was a great grandma, hands on and wanting to help.

Our easy adjustment to family life with one child prompted us to eagerly tell our social worker we wanted another child: a little girl "one year from now." We once again stepped into a place of control. We wanted our daughter by September. We were building a new home that was going to be ready by June. By September we would be ready to welcome our second child. The agency updated our file.

By fall the Monday morning adoption agency calls started coming again. Mrs. Font would call to report things, like, "There was a girl but she had red hair so I didn't take her for you!" Ouch! She was not very open to possibilities, as she made all the decisions and didn't ever give us a chance to decide whether or not red hair was acceptable for us! We felt like she was playing God's role in our lives.

Just one month later, in October, the call came telling us we had been accepted as parents for a baby daughter. We were told to come to receive her at the agency on Wednesday at 10 a.m., two days later.

We were told our 3-month-old daughter was very shy, and advised to proceed cautiously when approaching her in the nursery. They did not want us to startle her. Mandy was in a little swinging cradle. Jason, now twenty-two months old, ran ahead of us to see the baby. He leaned into the cradle and it began to swing! We rushed to calm the cradle and get our first glance at our new daughter. There was Mandy smiling, almost laughing, in her cradle. She didn't seem shy at all and we were so glad Jason had not frightened her. Mandy was so cute. She was bald, pink cheeked, with a darling dimple in the middle of her chin. We changed her into the new yellow outfit we had brought along, took pictures, and rushed home. Again the phone rang incessantly, everyone eager to meet our newest family member. The first night in our home Mandy slept all night. Mandy was a very good baby, happy and playful. Mandy ate well, and seemed to adjust very readily to her new family but she wasn't very cuddly. This was our first sign of her independence.

The brief note we got from Mandy's foster parents was very factual and cold. Sadly there were no personal anecdotes about her, only the facts.

Our new home had been completed four months before Mandy's arrival. We felt blessed, and content. I rejoiced, "Now, we are really a family! A boy for you and a girl for me, ready to live happily ever after."

4

Foster Daughters: Krista and Katie

During these early months of settling in with Jason and Mandy, Terry and I met Krista while teaching a ninth grade catechism class at our church. Krista's dad had died when she was only two, leaving her mom to raise six kids alone! Krista was orphaned when her mom died three years earlier of pneumonia, complications from Hong Kong flu. When Krista's mom died, her paternal uncle's family had stepped in to care for the three girls while the three brothers went to live with family friends on the other side of town.

Krista was a very sweet darling vibrant girl and we really liked her. We asked her to babysit Jason and Mandy for us. Krista was an excellent babysitter. She was cute, friendly, and seemed to really like our two children. The feeling was mutual. We always felt so fortunate when Krista was available and could babysit for us. We hired Krista almost every weekend. It was a long drive back to where she lived at her Aunt's house. During our drives Krista shared with me her struggles living with her aunt and uncle who already had six children and now they had added Krista and her two sisters to their family.

One evening while driving Krista home after babysitting I casually suggested, "If you ever need a break from your Aunt's home, you can come stay with us for a weekend. Maybe a little space now and then would do you both some good."

Not long after that I received a phone call from County Social Services asking if we would consider taking Krista Barret into our home on a long-term basis. Our names had been given to the social worker as a possible resource. I laughed saying, "There was some mistake." I explained, "We told Krista she could come some *weekend* for a visit. That was all!"

The worker told me, "The aunt is exhausted and needs the girls to move *now!*"

"*Girls?*"

"Yes, Krista's sister Katie also has to move. She is one year older."

I was speechless.

She continued, "The third and eldest sister has already left the aunt's home."

I fumbled to explain, "I will talk to Terry about this and get back to you."

Many thoughts raced through my head. I told the social worker, "We will call you back on Monday."

Terry and I had made all the arrangements to go on a married couple's retreat that weekend. We sure couldn't make any changes over the weekend.

Talk and prayer throughout the weekend led us to believe we could, and should take these girls into our family. Would we be able to be a family with *four* children, two teenagers and two young children? Being young and eager for the family of our dreams we did not have the maturity to realize Mandy had only been with us for seven months and was still adjusting to her new home. Jason was only two years old.

We decided we loved children, and had the means to care for them. We could do it.

We invited both girls the following Wednesday, to come to our home for dinner so Katie could meet our two children for the first time. Both girls were darling, we were idealistic, and so began our journey and love relationship with Krista and Katie. We accepted them as "our daughters."

So *now* the stage is set for the "happy family," mom and dad, two teens, and two toddlers. We went camping and boating, doing all we knew to be a close family. We tried our best to meet the emotional needs of our growing family, with the added stress of raising teens and toddlers together. I felt assured that loving our children would be all we needed to do.

Mandy was only eleven months old when the girls moved in. There was more change and challenge than I had expected for all of us. In retrospect I admit that I was very anxious. I found it exhausting to now be parenting teens *and* toddlers at the same time. Back then I thought of myself as "high energy" not stressed; but, Terry did occasionally find me crying in bed at night, because I felt like I wasn't doing a "good enough" job with the four children.

Krista and Katie were good girls. They obeyed our rules, had friends, and were doing the normal teenage things. Terry and I thought because we were young ourselves, just 28 and 29, we would have instant rapport; but, protectiveness obsessed us. We thought we were so close to their ages that we could understand them. We had no idea what raising these orphaned girls should entail. Being good friends was not enough as these girls had been abandoned by dying parents and needed so much love and attention. They had barely started grieving the loss of their parents, and now they had to struggle again to adapt to new people and new surroundings.

Nine months after they moved into our home, Jason was hospitalized with spinal meningitis. The doctors took a week before they diagnosed the problem. Jason was hospitalized three weeks. This time was very traumatic for all of us. Krista and Katie were very agitated about Jason being in the hospital. They had not gone to the hospital when their mother was dying, but they knew she was in the hospital when she died. We felt it was important for them to visit Jason in the hospital and learn that everyone that goes to the hospital does not die. The girls visited Jason in the hospital once after he was stabilized and in recovery. After this long month of major concern with Jason's health we settled back into a *normal* living routine.

One issue we quickly realized and had to face was the fact that boys liked Krista! She was vivacious, flirty, and buxom. Krista was built like a Barbie doll and also naïve of her effect on boys. I'd take her downstairs at night for "talks". I'd say, "Honey you have to be careful how friendly you are with all the boys." She would look at me blankly and say she didn't know what I meant. She truly got along better with guys than girls, thinking girls were caddy and backbiting. As the months wore on the task of raising four children wore us down. I was plagued with doubts because I didn't always *feel* loving toward Krista, now that she lived with us. I was frustrated because I did not seem to connect with her and her needs. I wanted everyone happy and didn't know how to *make* them that way. I didn't have the maturity to understand that love is spelled "commitment" with teenagers, and that even biological birth moms didn't *feel* loving all the time, either.

My frustration with my relationship with Krista turned into depression. After much counsel with the social worker and much soul searching we decided Krista had to leave our home. She had to move out. I felt so much pressure and responsibility that it was straining our marriage. I couldn't be happy if the girls weren't happy. I felt like we could never have everyone on the same page at the same time. I was trying to *fix* everyone. Krista was doing her own thing, and did not listen to what I had to say. She was independently trying to find herself and meet her own needs the way she knew how. Hindsight helps me realize she was starved for attention and trying to get it wherever she could.

At this same time, I was once again deeply involved with my younger sister Tess. As mentioned earlier, Tess had been troubled as a child and had gone to a school for special needs children by the age of 8. Tess was my sister with "mental illness," and our family was vigilantly concerned for her and her second child, now 3 years old. I was concerned about inappropriate care of the child, so I was trying to help in this situation. Tess now had another guy in her life within months of her divorce. She was struggling emotionally with unstable behavior. We all remembered the death of her first baby. My older sister filed abandonment charges with the county against Tess, after she had left her baby at my sister's home for two weeks.

The pressures at home had also escalated at this time to the point where the social worker, Terry and I felt that one or both of the girls had to leave our home as the situation was more than I could handle emotionally. In an attempt to help me deal with these stressors in my life we had a meeting with the foster girls and the social worker. Terry and I felt like failures because we realized we were wounding those we had committed to love. Terry, Krista, Katie and I were all crying as we sat together at the kitchen table. The social worker held her tears back and left with the burden of the decision of what to do with the foster care situation for Krista.

Jason was 3½ and Mandy was soon to be 2. Were the two children taking naps as we sat around the table? It is significant to me that I don't even remember where the kids were as we talked or whether or not we had later told them what had happened regarding Krista's absence from our home.

Krista had to leave and Katie was told it was her choice to stay or go with Krista. Krista went to live with a girlfriend's family; but Katie chose to stay with us. While Krista was living with us, Katie was an introvert, quiet and withdrawn. Later we realized she had been depressed, which was indicated by her sitting and staring out the window by the hour. How my heart bled for her. Katie had now lost the rest of her family: her four older siblings earlier and now her younger sister/best friend. I felt so inept attempting to help these girls with their very obvious pain. After Krista left our home, we saw quite a transformation in Katie. She blossomed and became more self-assured and open. She stayed in our home until she graduated from high school.

My personal opinion is that taking only one child at a time affords more time to connect emotionally with each child and not deal with sibling rivalry for attention.

5

Abandonment & Grief

The issues involved in adoption and foster parenting are complex. Children need nurture and love to feel secure and safe in a family but we were quite naïve thinking love was enough. We have since read many books on adoption, and learned what a complex transaction of the heart it is. Some of the resources I read are listed in Addendum C of this book. Each had value in educating us about some aspect of adoption.

It took about six years for us to forgive each other and heal our relationship with Krista. Krista was very gracious to forgive us. Krista got pregnant in her early twenties. The father refused to marry her, so Krista worked very hard to care for herself and her child. We invited Krista to come home and live for about four months so she could save money for an apartment.

One evening we were up late talking about the loss of her dad at such an early age and the impact it had on her. Terry and I had just completed a course at our church on praying with people for inner healing of wounded hearts and spirits. As we talked I felt the Lord speak to my heart that Krista needed to forgive her daddy for leaving her. She was two years old when he died. Krista said, "Josie, that's silly. I know daddy didn't want to leave us." (Her father had died of leukemia at age 33.) She started to sob, and then, by faith, she prayed to forgive her father for leaving her.

At that moment she began to scream the most blood-curdling scream I had ever heard, from the depths of her soul. I believe that at that time she was set free from the deep grief from the loss of her father. Krista seemed more lighthearted and free after that time. She has always been able to minister to people, out of a deep mercy and love in her heart. I believe it is a direct result of her healing of a broken heart that evening. God did what no man could do; touch Krista's soul with His comfort.

This is what I think biblical deliverance looks like. It doesn't have to be a big power struggle of demonic forces, but an authoritative gentle prayer directed to God's heart to take over in a situation. Forgiving someone, alive or dead, can set us free to love the way God intended. We have watched the girls heal, slowly but surely over time, owning their grief, processing their anger and abandonment, and releasing it to God. It has been a forty-year process for them.

Abandonment is the central core of damage for those who have been adopted and/or placed in foster care. A child cannot comprehend the loss of those they "know" even in the uterus. When a child's parents die and leave them alone the child flounders unable to understand the whys, whats or whens of their losses. Hurt and pain of such an indefinable loss cannot be expressed, as the child has no understanding or words with which to explain their feelings. They just feel. Many adopted individuals have this pervasive sense of grief they do not even know how to name or understand which colors their life until they can face it and gain some understanding about their loss.

Those who have experienced the loss of loved ones as adults have an idea how the child must feel, but as adults we also have some words to use to explain our feelings. The child does not. The feelings often erupt as anger with cries or screams of anguish from a non-verbal infant.

Becoming an instant parent of teenagers is definitely a difficult step for anyone. Parenting a child from infancy gives the parents a chance to know the child before attempting to assist a teenager though those volatile teen years. During the teen years the teenager must deal with the stretching and challenging choices in their attempts to grow into independence and the self-responsibility of adulthood, along with adjusting to the hormonal body changes of adulthood. The years of nurturing a child through their early years are years for the parents to learn to love their uniqueness and how to develop a working relationship of caring and communicating. Jumping into the midst of "teenage troubles" is truly like jumping into hot boiling water. Remember the frog can be boiled to death if you start with cold water and turn up the heat, but if you dump him into the boiling water the frog will instantly jump out of the pot!

Josie was realizing her inadequacies in attempting to parent two teenagers, both deeply wounded by the loss of their parents and their siblings, their known life, when she chose to make changes for the foster daughters. With no earlier years together, foster parents do not have an awareness of the history, the damages of neglect and/or abuse the child has lived through. They have no knowledge of the relationships from those years, which may have nurtured or damaged the child. There are so many voids in the parenting relationship with the child that it may seem like an impossible task to grasp and know what and how to relate to the older child.

My impression is that grief is a huge part of the adoption adjustment. Children do not have any words to describe what is happening in their hearts. If a person is willing to acknowledge their loss and grieve it they can move forward unencumbered in life. The grieving process is difficult but without it we sentence ourselves to carry the burden and pain for the rest of our lives. It is a choice to deny or face the reality of the loss experienced.

6

Our Family Grows

By the time Mandy turned two I could not keep her in her crib for a nap. I definitely did not understand the term "power struggle" even though I lived it every day. Many times a day I put her back in her bed to rest, but she would climb out. Our older son had taken his nap without incidence until age five, so this was hard for me to understand. Mandy challenged our authority as soon as she could and it continued for years. Every babysitter we had would tell us she was hard to handle, not listening to the instructions. At that time Attention Deficit Hyperactive Disorder (ADHD) was not a common diagnosis. We are now sure that was the challenge we faced with Mandy.

Mandy's early years were difficult, yet I was always sure peace was right around the corner. Jason turned five, and Mandy was four years old. Our home was quiet, and I began to think the timing was right for us to continue with our plan to have six children. We knew Katie would be leaving our home within the next six months following her graduation.

Katie graduated in June and was eager to get her own apartment. We told her we expected her to get a part-time job. She reacted with angry pouting, but did comply. Looking back I believe she was afraid rather than unwilling to work. By January, Katie and two of her high school classmates found an apartment to share.

Terry and I talked back and forth for several months after Katie left our home about the possibility of adopting a third child. Terry said that since we already had one boy and one girl he could see no reason to continue. I finally told him the application forms for another adoption were in my dresser drawer, if he should ever change his mind.

Five months after leaving our home Katie's roommates came to tell us Katie was acting "strange." I called her inviting her to visit soon. Within a couple of weeks Katie came over with her friends and while we all chatted, she jokingly asked, "Wouldn't it be crazy if one of us girls got pregnant?" A big joke, an imaginary scenario, it was just a general discussion, or so we thought.

Within a week she was back at our home telling us *she* was seven months pregnant. We were stunned. Her siblings had nicknamed Katie "the queen of denial." And *she* had not even *suspected* she was pregnant. When she went to the doctor she was surprised when he told her she was pregnant. *We* did not even know she had a boyfriend! We did not understand, but Katie's distancing from us now began to make sense. She acted as if she could confidently take care of herself and her child. We felt she did not want us involved in her life at this time. Katie's baby boy was born two months later just before Christmas.

Katie's baby boy was 3 weeks old when a man we had never met moved in with Katie. When we went to visit Katie's baby, a man was holding the baby. Katie introduced us, "This is my friend, Tom."

"Oh." We were startled, not knowing that Katie was dating any one at that time. We were realizing just how much Katie had kept from us.

As is our custom, our family went to Terry's parents' home for Christmas Eve dinner. That night Jason, our oldest son, developed a very severe case of croup. We were up with him all night. I had called the Doctor and he advised taking Jason into a very steamy shower and then out into the cold night air to open his airways. We thought the doctor was nuts but followed his counsel and Jason started to breath normally and went back to sleep. It was 5 a.m. when I dropped into bed exhausted from the stress and worry. I clearly remember crying to myself, "This cinches it; now, Terry will never want more kids, after all this worry and stress with a sick child."

Terry and I went to separate church services Christmas day, so one of us could be home with the children. About two in the afternoon Terry came to me and said he had another Christmas present for me; he wanted to sign the papers to apply for another child. I was stunned and delighted. Terry went on to say that he had sat behind a family in church that had a little baby. As he watched them, and saw their loving exchange, he wanted the same for us. He decided children were the most precious gift we could have from God, and why not have more!

We completed the adoption application immediately and sent it off to Family Services.

Right after Christmas, we quickly completed the paper work for another adoption. Shortly thereafter, the agency called to tell us we were not eligible for another Caucasian child because we already had the limit of two. We were encouraged to apply for a child of another race, such as African American or Korean. We went to an information meeting and decided to apply for a Korean child. Terry was more apprehensive about this than I was. He felt nervous about the unknowns. When the adoption file came from Korea, the agency called to say we could come review it. I was working part-time as a social worker at the time, so Terry took off and ran over to the office to get the baby's picture. We named the baby Chad. The photo made me giggle, because Chad's complexion was so dark, and his little face seemed so flat and so cute. Chad was even cuter in person; the photo did not do him justice.

Jason was five and Mandy was four as we prepared for the arrival of Chad, our third child, our second adopted son.

Each time I announced another adoption plan my own mom would say to me, "Are you *sure* you want to do this?" Having raised eight children, I know my mom was trying to gently caution us about the many possible cares of parenting in the years ahead of us.

We only waited five months before our little boy Chad arrived at five thirty on a Thursday evening. We were filled with anticipation and joy. We invited friends and relatives to join us at the airport for his arrival. The arrival time was delayed an hour so we scurried to inform all the people. This was before the days of cell phones and text messaging, so we assigned a friend to try to contact everyone about the delay. It all worked out although it added additional stress. Our beautiful little son seemed overwhelmed with all the faces staring at him and hands reaching out for him. Chad sucked his fingers and clicked his tongue all the way from the airport terminal to our home, as if he was saying, "Yikes this is a lot. I'll just play it cool!"

For the first three weeks Chad rarely smiled, until my brother came and greeted him, "Chaddy me boy!" Chad broke out into a broad smile and from then on he smiled frequently. Chad settled in well, slept through the night, and seemed to adjust quickly to the new family with two eager siblings hovering over him all day. Terry and I were delighted with our son; there's no other way to describe it. Chad was so sweet, cuddly, pleasant and mellow. One evening that fall we were walking around the block after dinner and Terry said to me, "We're going to get Chad a little sister in about a year!" This was such an easy decision, after the weighty time of making the decision to have a third child. Wow! I was thrilled to pieces not having to wait for our fourth child. We were in total agreement. Chad had only been in our home for four months at the time of this decision.

Chad was definitely our compliant, easy to raise child. He was reserved, had a sense of humor, and was very obedient. He was the child who would receive correction with "a look" in his direction and he'd obey.

When Chad was one year old we implemented our plan for a fourth child. We applied for a Korean baby girl ~ family planning at its finest: boy-girl, boy-girl! I guess we did not think about sharing bedrooms. The seven-month wait went quickly. This time we decided to avoid confusion for the arrival of this baby so we took only our children and Terry's parents with us to the airport.

Our fourth child Jenna joined our family two years after our son Chad had come from Korea. Jenna was an adorable petite baby with lots of black hair and dimples. She adjusted very well. We were so happy to have Jenna home with us. Terry adored her and she him. Jenna was a sweet, very shy child, who followed Terry wherever he went. Her siblings loved to touch and be by her. The family videotapes show the children swarming around her, big brother Jason smothering her with kisses. Jenna settled in easily sleeping through the night.

When Jenna was one, Chad 3, Mandy 7 and Jason 9 we bought a lake cabin for our family's summer fun. The place had a great beach for the children. The cabin was run-down and needed lots of TLC, but we took time out regularly to play with the children in the water. We have great winter memories, too, when we ice-skated on the frozen lake one New Year's eve.

We became born-again Christians when Jenna was two years old. We learned that God could and would heal people of infertility. Terry and I began going into prayer lines at church asking for prayer for conception of a child. We believed God could do this miracle for us. One morning at the cabin Terry came to me with the report of a dream-like experience he had. He thought he heard the Lord ask him, "Which of your children do you not want?" Terry was puzzled and replied, "Lord, I want all of my children."

Then he felt the Lord said in reply, "Then who are you to tell me how I am to give them to you?"

We felt this was our answer and we realized we would not have a pregnancy, so when Jenna was two years old we called Family Social Service and asked them if they would accept a fifth application from us. In my heart of hearts I felt there was one more child "out there" who was supposed to be a member of our family. They said we were now at their *limit*: two Caucasian children and two foreign born children per family. At that time Jason was 10, Mandy 8, Chad, 4 and Jenna was 2.

Terry came from work one evening, excited about an advertisement he had heard on the radio promoting a new Christian adoption agency. He suggested I call them the next day. The social worker was very encouraging to us, saying they would gladly take an application for a bi-racial child. She explained that their agency had placed three bi-racial babies in the last three weeks. We were amazed and very encouraged about this news.

We had to start all over with the home study process since this was a new agency. Terry and I had to write an autobiography as part of the process. I really recommend everyone take the time to do this sometime in life. It was a good exercise in reviewing my life and reevaluating my goals. Terry and I both enjoyed the assignment. I remember being surprised at some of the things Terry wrote that I didn't know about him. It always amazes me how we can live with someone for so long, and continue to learn new things about them along life's way. It makes marriage very special and intimate.

There was one major stumbling block for me in this adoption, which was causing me to feel guilty. Terry seemed totally open to a bi-racial child. But I, on the other hand, started to fret about how to take care of a black child's hair. I was trying to keep it to myself, but God knew I was struggling with the thought and fear of not being able to love the child. What should be a minor thing became major to me. I decided to not go ahead until this was resolved in my heart, because I did not want any emotional barrier between my child and myself.

As new born-again Christians we were just learning the Bible. The Bible came alive for us. We found joy, comfort and direction while reading the Bible. What happened next deepened my faith in the power of the Word of God to direct our steps and calm our hearts. I read:

> "Which of you, if your son asks for bread will give him a stone? Or if he asks for a fish, will give him a snake? If you, then, though you are evil, know how to give good gifts to your children, how much more will your Father in heaven give good gifts to those who ask Him!" Matthew 7:9-11

My spirit leaped for joy. God was reassuring me that He would not give me a child I couldn't love. Father was assuring me the hair would not be a stumbling block for me. I share this story to show how God cares about every detail of my life and how the Word has been a compass for me. I have never had any situation where the Bible didn't have some comfort or guidance for me.

We rushed through the screening process. The social worker said we would have a baby within the next two months. We hurried home and set up a nursery for our newest family member. Each week we waited for the call. One month led to two months and on to three months. I'd call periodically to make sure they hadn't forgotten us. The social worker said there simply were no expectant mothers who fit the bi-racial criteria, since we had applied. She was very apologetic, but assured us God had a plan for us. Two years went by and finally I spoke to the social worker about applying to another agency and she strongly encouraged us to do so.

Terry and I talked and decided to call Family Services back again, since they had all our records from our four other children. To our surprise, the agency had changed their policy and would gladly take an application for a fifth child, our third from Korea. We were thrilled and filled out the paperwork immediately. This was in early February.

Our fifth child, a boy, was born that same month! We got his portfolio that spring and we named him Todd. He joined our family mid-summer that same year, only five months after the initial call.

We had our entire family and Bible study group at the airport. Todd was an adorable little baby, with a very round face, scant black hair sticking straight up, with a very happy playful personality. He was embraced and loved by our whole family. When we watch our home videos of him, we see he was smothered in attention from his siblings.

There was a five-year age gap between Todd and Jenna. The New Birth Order Book states when there is a five-year gap in ages the next child develops similar to another first born (Leman, 1999, pg. 22).

Todd was very energetic and busy, always moving, climbing, and talking. I needed a lot of energy to keep up with him. We enjoyed him so much, but I got tired of constantly checking on him to see where he was and what he was doing. Friends would quip to me that Todd was "overly present" because he never sat still. He was obedient; he just never stayed focused on anything for any length of time. It was because of this that Terry decided, "If anyone asks us Todd's name we'll say 'we call him quits' because we wouldn't be having a sixth child." We acknowledged that five children was now our new limit for our family. We were now 38 and 40 years old respectively, so obviously that had something to do with our energy level. We couldn't place our energy drain all on our active little boy!

When we were waiting for Todd to come home a friend had said how glad she was that we were having a baby and *not* her. Many people seemed to be critical of us as we added a fifth child to our family. One friend Joan had said, "You just know when you are done having children and I know I'm done!" I guess she thought we should be done, too! We thought we had things under control and it was none of her business!

Life was very busy but very enjoyable with our five children: Mom and Dad, Jason 12, Mandy 10 ½, Chad 7, Jenna 5 and new baby Todd. I enjoyed Todd's pleasant personality so much. Todd was totally extroverted, obedient and he loved being around people. Our family was now complete. The children were growing and we were able to do many outdoor activities together: hockey, soccer, swimming, and downhill skiing all together as a family by the time Todd was 4!

Terry worked hard and God blessed his efforts financially. We were able to go and do many things together. The adoption agency worker had told us near the beginning of the adoption process that she had never seen an adoptive family have financial troubles. We have never forgotten what she said. God blessed us as we opened our home to His children.

7

I Was Adopted

I was upset with my neighbor Ginger and decided to go clear the air because I felt she had been badgering me about needing *Jesus* in my life. I, on the other hand, was trying to persuade her and her hubby to make a Marriage Encounter Weekend. Terry and I were leaders in Marriage Encounter and I could tell their marriage was struggling. Whenever I'd invite her she'd tell me I needed Jesus. I thought she was very arrogant. On this day in July I planned to settle this once and for all.

I was saying bedtime prayers with Jason the night before when he prayed that God would make me more loving, like Ginger. Ouch, that hurt, but I totally knew what he meant. Ginger's words were always kind, gentle and full of life. So this day I went to her, wanting to have a heart-to-heart talk with her.

We chatted a little and then I asked Ginger again about Marriage Encounter. I was as stubborn as she was! She gave me her usual answer, "Josie, you need Jesus!" I bristled and proceeded to tell Ginger all I *did* for God: teaching catechism, helping build our church building, serving in every way I knew how.

Ginger smiled, "Josie, you know God here," as she pointed to her head, then pointing to her heart she said, "But you don't know Him here."

I asked what she meant. Ginger said I needed to be born again, to personally thank Jesus for dying for me, and ask Him to take control of my life, and come live in my heart. I said, "OH, I can do that. I believe everything you're saying."

So I held her hand, confessed I was a sinner, and asked Jesus to come take over control of my entire life, to forgive my sins, and to make me into the person he wanted me to be for His glory.

I was adopted into God's family on July 10th, 1979, at 1:10 p.m. while sitting at my neighbor's kitchen table. That was the very day I became a Child of God, because I deliberately invited Jesus to take control of my life. Jesus spoke to Nicodemus about his need to be born again. Nicodemus asked Jesus how it was possible; could a person enter their mother's womb again? Jesus replies:

> "Very truly I tell you, no one can enter the kingdom of God unless they are born of water and the Spirit." John 3:5

That was the beginning of the wonderful journey for the rest of my life.

> "In love He predestined us for adoption to sonship through Jesus Christ, in accordance with His pleasure and will, to the praise of His glorious grace, which He has freely given us, in the One He loves." Ephesians 1:5-6
>
> "In other words, it is not the natural children who are God's children, but it is the children of the promise who are regarded as Abrahams' offspring." Romans 9:8
>
> "I will call them my people who are not my people; I will call her my loved one who is not my loved one; and it will happen in the very place where it was said to them, you are not my people that they will be called sons of the living God." Romans 9:25-26

God is saying here that He will take me, who has no claim or inheritance from Him, and He will graft me into Him, making me a part of His family. This is adoption: taking someone from a different heritage and assimilating them into our family, engrafted, giving them our family inheritance.

> "Because those who are led by the Spirit of God are sons of God. For you did not receive a spirit that makes you a slave again to fear but you received the spirit of sonship. And by Him we cry Abba Father. The Spirit Himself testifies with our spirit that *we are God's children*." Romans 8:14-16
>
> "We know that the whole creation has been groaning as in the pains of *childbirth* right up to the present time. Not only so, but we ourselves who have first fruits of the Spirit, groan inwardly as we wait eagerly for our *adoption* as sons, the redemption of our bodies." Romans 8:22-23

I await my glorified resurrection body promised to me because of my adoption into God's family.

There are some days that I am more painfully aware than others that I am spiritually adopted, as I try to "work out my salvation with fear and trembling" (Philippians 2:12). I choose to die to my fleshly desires and walk in God's ways in my personal life. My human nature is so different than the supernatural character of God, who lives in my heart. I need to die to bitterness, anxiety, resentment, and all the other natural tendencies I inherited as part of being human. I must purpose to act in the nature of my Heavenly Father who has adopted me into His family through my confession of faith in Him.

Paul clearly defines the crisis of the Christian life in Romans.

"I know that nothing good lives in me that is my sinful nature. For I have the desire to do what is good, but I cannot carry it out." Romans 7:18

"Therefore, there is now no condemnation for those who are in Christ Jesus, because through Christ Jesus the law of the Spirit of life has set me free from the law of sin and death." Romans 8:1-2

These scriptures state my adoption into God's family gives me a *new* inheritance in Jesus Christ, *not* the law of sin and death into which I was naturally born. Praise God for His remarkable plan to all who choose Him.

Can you say this day:

"Jesus, I am a sinner. I need a Redeemer to set me free from this law of sin and death. I accept what Jesus did on Calvary to pay for my sins, and I want to be adopted into your family this day." If your answer is yes, pray to your Father, and mark your spiritual birthday in your Bible. Jesus clearly tells Nicodemus he won't understand the kingdom of God unless he enters it and the only way to enter is through the new birth in Christ.

Since the day that I prayed this prayer, I know I have taken on more of my heavenly Father's character and attributes, laying aside my human condition. God has been growing me up as His child, to reflect His life to those around me. I gossip less, don't stay angry as long, and have a grateful heart for the small things of life. Each of us can become like a blossoming flower, when we yield our will over to His control.

My genetic lineage or sin-nature as a human being can be changed as I let Christ have His way in my life. That is some trade isn't it? My sorrow and shame for His riches and glories in Christ Jesus!

> "How great is the love the Father has lavished on us that we should be called children of God." 1 John 3:1a

That is who we are!

Each of us must choose daily, moment-by-moment, and choice by choice to do things God's way. To fight addictions of substances, emotions, and perversions we have been involved in, we must fight the battle over and over again, until the spiritual forces working against us give up and know without a doubt we are committed to following after God's way. We must know in our own hearts that we must live and choose His way to walk in it. As we surrender He can even change our desires!

Since that day of my adoption I have had the privilege of praying with many people to invite Jesus Christ to be their Lord and Savior. It is one of my greatest joys to invite someone to join the family of God through spiritual adoption.

The process is very similar to physical adoption. I allowed myself to be *grafted* into the vine of the heritage of Jesus Christ's nature in order to be a member of the family of God. Adopted children must allow themselves to be grafted into the adoptive family, taking on their new family's identity. They must allow themselves to give and receive the love of their parents. Just as all my children are the ones to inherit our assets, so I get to inherit the assets of God, as I become a member of His family. I must be willing to love God and let Him love me back.

> "Christ in you, the hope of glory." Colossians 1:27b

42

We can find in the gospel of John, the word picture of us being the branch and Christ as the vine from which we get our growth.

> "Remain in me and I will remain in you. No branch can bear fruit by itself; it must remain in the vine. Neither can you bear fruit unless you remain in Me. I am the vine; you are the branches. If a man remains in Me and I in him he will bear much fruit; apart from me you can do nothing." John 15:4-5

In the natural world, adopted children must allow themselves to be "grafted" into the new family line. The more our children want to be a "Jones," to emulate our values and our character qualities, the more unity there will be in the home. There is a constant tension in the adopted person's heart to be an individual, wanting to find his or her own way, separate from us, and being part of the family. Truly all children, biological or adopted, must do this eventually. It seems to me that some of my children have chosen some of their birth parents' values, rather than the Jones' values. It is their choice. My challenge is to love and accept each of them as a unique, special gift to me, loaned from God, for a season of my life. The tension of blending different traits has been far more challenging than I ever imagined. I gave little consideration to each child bringing their unique natures of their birth families into the Jones family. I was in denial and unprepared for the realities inherent in adoption and intensified in cross-cultural adoption.

Open adoption is when birth and adoptive parents meet before the birth, and the adoptive parents may be present at the birth of the child. The meeting of these individuals may help the adoptive parents understand the differences between the biological family and the adoptive family. These observations may help the adoptive parents understand and accept the differences between the two families, ultimately helping them parent their adopted child.

We ignored the influence of the birth families' contribution of nature, genetic influence. We felt our nurturing was all that was necessary for each child we brought home. Would I do it again? Unequivocally, yes! Would I be more realistic, unequivocally yes; after our years of parenting I now see my children are a blend of their genetic inheritance and the influence of our nurturing. The blending of nature and nurture within an adopted child may cause an inner conflict that the child can't define but makes it more difficult for the child to identify and accept who they are.

The age-old argument of heredity vs. environment, or nature vs. nurture, is part of every child's development but particularly that of the adopted child. These are two strong influences that help to determine who each child becomes.

We are identifiable with our family lineage by our DNA. Sons and daughters have very similar DNA to their parents. DNA can be studied through blood and other tissues. Are the eyes going to be nearsighted or farsighted? Will a hearing loss crop up as old age approaches? Is there a missing chromosome within the DNA chain that will probably cause a particular disease to develop? Many more characteristics and determinates are being discovered.

Our environment can be explained as the modeled behavior of the people around us in the home as we grow up: those who are parents, extended family, teachers and friends. People have an influence on one another. "No man is an island," explains the fact that we all are changed by the contact and experiences we have with others throughout our walk of life.

Which is stronger our genetic disposition, i.e. heredity, or the environmental influences of our journey? Only God knows!

8

Troubled Waters

Now we were a family with five beautiful children: Jason 12, Mandy 11, Chad 7, Jenna 5 and Todd 1. We were enjoying life doing many family activities, reveling in our newfound faith in God. As our oldest children started their teenage years our lives became more challenging.

Jason was involved in many high school activities and did well academically. He pushed our limits but generally made wise choices. We enjoyed getting to know his many friends whom he brought to our home.

When Mandy was twelve years old she had what we understood to be an emergency appendectomy. She had normal post-surgical healing until about six weeks following the appendectomy. One sunny Saturday afternoon after coming home from the grocery store, I found Mandy crying in her room.

"I have a really bad headache." She told me, "It hurt so bad I went to the kitchen and anointed myself with oil, then prayed for God to heal me like we read people did in the Bible." Mandy went on, "Then I felt like someone was trying to choke me!"

I had Mandy come lay on my bed and I prayed for her. I went to Terry wondering what we should do next. By the time Terry and I returned up to the bedroom Mandy was writhing on the bed, thrashing, holding her throat saying, "They are trying to kill me!"

We immediately called the paramedics and then called our closest friends asking them to pray for us.

The 911 team of a policeman and two paramedics were unable to take Mandy's pulse; they could not hold her down. They decided they had to transport her but struggled to get her strapped down on the gurney. We were praying our hearts out, while trying to calm her as they took her to the ambulance. I rode to the hospital in the ambulance with Mandy. On the way to the hospital she calmed down but reported the headache was still unbearable. Our friends had contacted many others who by this time were also praying for us.

The doctors did brain scans, x-rays and many blood tests, all of which came back negative. Mandy said she had an upset stomach and then proceeded to vomit two bowls of green slimy phlegm. After that she reported she felt, "Fine."

Since the doctors could find nothing, they sent us home telling us to watch her closely. This episode seemed to change Mandy's disposition for the better. What had this all been about? She now was happy and cooperative. We felt she finally seemed to accept that she was lovable, a part of the family and did not appear to feel rejected all the time. I believe Mandy had experienced a very real *deliverance* in that hospital room, through all the prayers offered for her by our friends. We witnessed God heal Mandy in that hospital room.

Mandy's change in attitude lasted for about three weeks. Then gradually she seemed to revert back to her former ways of thinking and relating to others. Once again she was uncooperative, easily wounded and felt rejected.

[Mandy was thirty-three years old when she told me what this had all been about. She related that as a twelve year old, she had asked Satan to give her an appendix attack so she could have surgery. Mandy had observed one of her classmates who got a lot of attention when she

47

went to the hospital for an appendectomy. Mandy had wanted to get the attention but had not believed Satan would actually make her sick. At age 40 the adult Mandy had another encounter with Satan and this time commanded Satan to leave her alone. Earlier that evening, I had been at Bible study and asked for prayer for Mandy to have a real encounter with the Lord. She called me at midnight to tell me she now knew she had been duped at age 12, but this time she recognized what she had done, allowing Satan to take control and wreck her life all these years!]

The summer after her appendectomy, when Mandy was thirteen, we heard the rumors going around our neighborhood. Mandy had sneaked out of the house, and crawled into the neighbor boys' tent where they were having a sleepover. It was reported that she had sex with one of the boys.

When we confronted her she shrugged it off saying, "So, what's the big deal? Most of my friends aren't virgins and I wanted to be like them!"

I was hysterical inside, trying to remain calm on the outside. We contacted a pastor who worked well with youth and had him come to our home to speak with Mandy about the situation. The pastor and we tried to explain to Mandy the consequences of this behavior, with pregnancy, reputation, medical risks; he explained how boys are willing to engage girls for this favor for their pleasure. Mandy remained distant and seemed unmoved by any of the discussion.

We then went to a Christian counselor recommended through a local church who was a specialist with teens. He led us, the parents, through soul searching prayer about our own lives, trying to get at the root of our own childhood struggles. (This seemed strange to us, but we were willing to do whatever we could to help get Mandy through this and restore some peace to our family.) We confessed every sin of bitterness or rebellion against our own parents we could think of. We believe "the sins of the father can be passed on to the children to the 3rd and 4th generations," becomes a generational curse. We methodically made a list of all our known sins in each of Terry and my families. We also made a list of what we knew could be the sins in Mandy's birth parents generational line.

We prayed asking God to forgive us and break these generational curses off our family so that God would be glorified in our family. Some of the things I addressed from my family were alcoholism, lust, mental illness, and rejection. In Terry's family line we addressed alcoholism, lust, anger, and bitterness. Some obvious ones in Mandy's background that we prayed to break the power of were lying, stealing, lust, and rejection. We believe the name of Jesus Christ, and that the power of His shed blood has the authority to break any curse in our inheritance. We saw no immediate change in Mandy's behavior, but we knew and believed that God heard our prayers. Mandy has choices. She has to determine within herself to accept God's help in her battle.

Mandy was out of control and we were living in a cycle of rebellious activities, clamping down and restraining her with consequences from her behavior, which would bring her to a place of cooperation. Then as soon as we started restoring some privileges she would start acting out again, lying to cover her behaviors, and soon she would be totally out of control again.

During this time as our parental focus was Mandy's behavior, Chad studied hard, got good grades, and was well liked by his friends. Chad was now twelve years old. One day Chad and I went shopping and he got caught shoplifting by the security guard. Chad had money in his pocket, yet had taken a fishing lure.

I asked him, "Why did you steal the lure when you had enough money in your pocket to buy it?"

He only shrugged his shoulders but said nothing.

Now, it seems glaringly apparent Chad wanted and needed some attention from us. He acted like we were the ones with a problem and did not understand why we were upset with him. It was his first time of openly defying us.

Around this same time I had been taking Chad bowling on Saturdays, purposed to have some one-on-one alone time with him individually. In his teen years he gave me a lot of joy because he was obedient, had a good attitude and did not make waves. I now realize that all the time and energy given to try to control Mandy resulted in Chad receiving less than his share of attention and nurturing.

Jenna began demanding attention by complaining about going to public school. She decided she wanted to home school her fifth grade year. Her cousins were home schooling and she liked the idea. I had home schooled Mandy before so I knew the commitment I was making. I agreed to home school Jenna. The year and a half that we home schooled together was good for Jenna and me. (Now I wonder if Jenna was asking for my time and attention that she needed in an appropriate manner.)

The summer before Mandy was going into her senior year of high school she was working at a dry cleaning shop. She didn't want to go for the weekend to the cabin with us. We really did not want to leave her home, but her brother Jason would be home, too. We trusted Jason and thought he'd have some influence over her choices. I think we both needed time away, so in a fog of denial, hoping these two teens would be obedient, we took the other children off for a weekend.

We pulled into our driveway after our trip to our cabin for the weekend and were greeted by our pretty, blond, happy smiling daughter Mandy. She ran to the van and surprised me with a big hug saying, "Oh, Mom! I missed you so much." I was a bit stunned, but was pleased to get such a warm welcome from Mandy.

Terry and I and the three younger kids started to unload the van. As I walked through the door to the lower level of our home I smelled the pungent odor of stale beer. I was barefoot, and noticed my feet were wet.

I asked, "Mandy, what happened while we were gone?"

Mandy started to explain, "Oh. I spilled some water on the floor.

"Do I smell beer?"

"No! It's water!"

I was furious. The "warm welcome" started to make sense…

How many lies can a mother take?

I walked into the lower level bathroom and noticed the light fixture was broken. There was a blood soaked towel on the bathroom floor. I went upstairs and found a bloody rag in Mandy's bedroom.

By now I was enraged, screaming, "Mandy! What went on? What happened while we were gone?"

My reaction elicited a defensive stance from Mandy. She started to explain, "The party just got out of hand." She replied, "Don't be so angry with me! Jason was in on it too!"

Jason had actually joined in with Mandy's plans. Leaving Jason and Mandy at home was one of those very poor decisions on our part as parents.

I totally lost control and started screaming at her to pick up the mess downstairs. This was an out of control moment as parents. Terry and I were both screaming at her, and telling her, "Get moving." Terry actually took her over his knee and spanked her. (To this day I regret and feel sad we were both out of control.) We had reached a point of total frustration. We were in the throes of craziness! We were undoubtedly mad at ourselves for leaving Mandy, now 17, and Jason, 19, at home alone for the weekend. Our worst fears had happened. And we did not know how to handle this situation. We felt like failures as parents, knowing this was partially our fault by leaving them unsupervised.

Mandy responded to our rage by running away. She left the house that night as we slept, called a cab, and went to a neighboring community. We traced her through some friends, called the police, and they met us where she was staying with two young men. She seemed very surprised to see us, but refused to come with us. By this time I was having great remorse for screaming at her. After all, I was a Christian, and had just come from a weekend of rest.

The police returned her to her girlfriend Sue's home, with our permission. Sue's mom was a Christian, and we knew she would be safe there.

We all needed to cool off emotionally to live in any kind of peace. Much later we learned what a devastating effect our behavior that night had on our other children. They had watched and listened. They were unforgiving toward us for a long time because of the way we railed at Mandy, yelling and screaming. This was one of many incidences that ravaged our life and family as we daily tried to control Mandy. We were frantic.

Why did we leave Mandy and Jason home alone? Jason finally admitted that he had been at the party also, and asked us to forgive him. He felt scared when the party got out of control, but he had not done anything to stop it!

During this time, Mandy had chummed with Barb, a girl we liked from our church. We felt Barb's friendship was a stabling influence for

Mandy. After the night of the wild party at our home Barb called to ask our forgiveness, for being a part of that scene. She said the party went beyond plans and got out of their control. Word had spread to a really wild bunch of kids who came knowing there was no adults at home. Mandy and Barb's friendship ended with that event.

My yelling and screaming was devastating, not helping. I had to learn to calm down, speak respectfully, and discipline in love, not anger. This awareness was a new focus for me, and took many trials to reach a place where I could respond in a constructive manner in these difficult situations. I wanted to be part of the solution not a part of the problem.

Much later we learned that Mandy had been sneaking out of the house in the middle of the night.

Chad knew something was going on and had actually loaned Mandy money that she used for her escapades. Chad normally was cooperative, funny, and reliable; however, during this time of Mandy's turmoil, Chad was very reserved. Chad stood by watching and assessing what was happening to our family. He was interpreting from the perspective of a thirteen year old; some of his conclusions have continued to affect his relationship with us, his parents. He has trouble trusting us and keeps his distance. The craziness in our family was affecting all of our relationships.

Finally, I contacted the nearby Adolescent Chemical Dependency Unit and asked them to evaluate Mandy because we suspected her behavior was tied to the use of alcohol and drugs. We had to coerce her to go to the counselor; we knew they were planning to keep her for five days, but we didn't tell her. We hated doing this, but we were desperate to know how to deal with her. We were afraid if we told her we were committing her for evaluation she would have run.

Our entire family met with a counselor, who prepared us for a time of intervention with Mandy. During the intervention Mandy had to remain silent while listening to her siblings talk about our home life. Several siblings said they hated the anger they saw in me toward her. I hated it too.

We had a meeting with the psychologist and several counselors at the end of Mandy's five days in the treatment program. The report indicated that Mandy's blood chemistry had actually changed because of her heavy use of alcohol. She had repeatedly lied in the group telling them she had never had more than one beer in her life. They said no one, especially the teens in the group, believed her.

The doctor did not recommend treatment, as Mandy wasn't ready to admit she needed help. He said he was afraid Mandy was someone who would have to learn life's lessons the hard way. The team told us we had been "saints" for putting up with her this long; but that we should release her to learn the hard lessons of the life she had chosen. We weren't saints by any means, but we were committed parents who loved our daughter the best way we knew how. We had hoped to help her find responsible and mature coping skills.

Mandy ran from our home the day she got out of the chemical evaluation unit and began living with the family of one of her friends. Mandy was seventeen. We knew the family because our children had attended the same school so we thought it was a safe place for her to live. The mom agreed to home school Mandy along with her seventeen year old daughter.

One night while Mandy was living at Sue's home, she called to chat saying she was going to a party later that evening. We were in the middle of a winter weather advisory, and a blizzard was raging. I asked Mandy not to drive because of the dangerous weather conditions. "Oh, Mom," was her response indicating I was too protective, over concerned. As I hung up, I was fearful for her life, and my eyes turned to the calendar on our wall with a picture of two sparrows on a branch with the words, "His eye is on the sparrow." It was a message from God, a rhema word, a comforting moment for me when Father God was speaking directly to my heart assuring me that He had Mandy's life in His hands. (The scripture verse is from Matthew 10:29 and has been a reminder for me many times of the assurance of His presence in our lives during our journey with Mandy.)

We ached for her as she repeatedly made friends who eventually would reject her. I don't think there is a mom alive who doesn't want to see her child happy and enjoying life, developing their God given skills. We were trying to help Mandy find the "keys" to peace and accountability so we could send her off to a productive and joyful life.

After that traumatic time, our foster daughter Krista came to me and asked me to check out Al-anon. Krista's husband had gone through rehab for alcohol addiction. Krista had attended Al-anon and had learned valuable lessons including clear communication skills. I was offended at first but decided I had nothing to lose and everything to gain if I could get a handle on my stress levels. What we had been doing had not been very successful and something needed to change.

I remember how I felt at my first Al-anon meeting. What I learned in the twelve-step meeting is that I was hurting not helping Mandy with what I thought was righteous anger. I learned that I am responsible to keep myself calm, and relate respectfully, no matter what the other person is doing, even if I am personally angered at their choices. These relational skills are actually scripturally based. My reactions had been based on my fears for her life and my desire to make her do what I wanted her to do. I needed Al-anon desperately. In the twelve-step group I began to learn to name and share my feelings without attacking others. I learned that my anger was uncontrolled reactive anger, not expressed appropriately. My anger was a typical reaction for a member of a chemically dependent family. An outsider often may judge the angriest family member as the problem rather than the user. I saw my anger as totally justified; after all, Mandy was the one breaking the rules.

> "…for man's anger does not work the righteousness of God." James 1:19b

Ouch, Jesus doesn't bash sinners with His tongue; He loves and woos them to repentance. I realized I was sinning as much as my child sinned by lying. It was the truth I needed to face and a behavior I needed to change.

I needed a lot of modeling of respectful conflict resolution before I understood how to do it. Al-anon was invaluable to me in teaching me how to be more nurturing, and communicate my feelings without condemning the other person. In the twelve-step group I learned to name and share *my* feelings without attacking others.

I have heard many Christians speak against AA, which was founded by God believing men who combined their study of scripture in the Oxford Group with the medical knowledge from Dr. Silkworth, who discovered that some people have an allergic reaction to alcohol, causing the body to become quickly addicted. In the book Alcoholics Anonymous 3rd addition, Bill W. co-founder of A.A. states, "There I humbly offered myself to God, as I then understood Him, to do with me as He would. I placed myself unreservedly under His care and direction. I admitted for the first time that of myself I was nothing; that without Him I was lost. I ruthlessly faced my sins, and became willing to have my new-found Friend take them away, root and branch. I have not had a drink since" (p. 13).

I did not have a conflict with my faith in the program. The groups were teaching me how to respectfully nurture and accept a person, and let them be responsible for their own actions, rather than feeling I had to fix them. Although, many people in twelve-step work have initially chosen a place, a song, or the group itself as their higher power, the program was founded with God and Jesus Christ as the Higher Power. I kept this at the forefront of my mind as people shared. In many ways twelve-step groups function more like the church Paul describes in the Book of Acts than most body of believers do today. Trust, forgiveness and fellowship are offered freely. The twelve steps can be seen as applied scripture. People are loved unconditionally and often respond positively to the nurturing they feel. The honesty and transparency is contagious.

Listening to others' problems, and how they dealt with them, helped me learn valuable lessons about nurturing. People accepted each other, no matter what was shared. In my own family, my mom and dad were not verbal. They talked very little to each other. I heard them argue, but never resolve a conflict. Mom complained about Dad to us. He stayed silent. They'd have flair ups, and then there would be a month long silence between them.

I learned that silence, ignoring another, is emotionally abusive. This silence was deafening and destructive. Silence may be considered pride, giving unspoken notice that I am right, and I will punish you by ignoring you as a person. Silence was also my mom's primary method of disciplining my brothers and sisters as we grew up, especially in the teen years. We all grew up and left our home feeling very insecure. We were always "on edge" about what was going to happen next.

Because I learned the silent treatment from my parents this became my usual response whenever Terry and I argued. I did what I had learned to do, even though I had vowed to myself I would never do the same. My behavior was what I knew. With God's help Terry and I have learned to talk things out to a place of resolution. I had to force myself to break the silence and begin talking to Terry about what I was thinking and feeling. Initially, the change in behavior patterns were very hard to do and very humbling, but became freeing for me as we learned how to talk about things. We had to practice as a couple so that we were able to openly communicate with our children. We still work at our communication skills and have by no means arrived at perfection.

Parental roles in caring for a rebellious and angry child are difficult. Parenting in such situations can be compared to triage work in an emergency care center. Words such as enabling, manipulating, co-dependency, disorders, and dysfunction all have a part when the relationships are malfunctioning. Triage in emergency situations is one of assessment. The damages are evaluated and those who can be assisted are given the most attention while those beyond help of recovery are given over to terminal care. Volatile teens may demand extra care and attention, but there is a line or boundary that must come into play in each relationship. When parents are over-protective or being manipulated beyond their comfort level to a place of resentment, the parents must realize something is out of control. Emergency assistance may be given, but then the experts should be called in to assist in the situation. The goal of parenting is to train and assist the child to a place of maturity where they can take care of themselves. There is a plaque with a picture of a kite flying off into the sky above which draws the analogy of "letting go" and letting the child go off on their own. Children are loaned to parents, whether birth parents or adoptive parents, for a time of care and nurturing until they are able to take care of themselves in all aspects of life.

Jenna's birth mom sent us her first letter from Korea when Jenna was only thirteen years old. It frightened me so much I almost disintegrated emotionally, sobbing, saying to the Lord, "No God, not now. We have too much going on with these kids." I felt engulfed in fear and recall sitting in our bathroom in a fetal position crying about the situation. I was afraid the mom would want to take Jenna away from us or that Jenna would want to go to her mother. I was so afraid because Jenna had become so emotionally fragile with the onset of puberty. We dealt with lots of angry outbursts from her. Or was it me I was worried about? Terry was very calm, and had just the right words to comfort and reassure me that no one would take Jenna from us.

We were right in the midst of many issues: Jason in his first year of college and meeting his birth parents, Chad dating and possibly sexually active, Mandy unmarried and pregnant.

The letter said that the birth mom went to the agency the day after she placed Jenna, and Jenna was already gone. The birth mom had deep regrets about placing Jenna who had lived at home with her birth mom the first two months of her life. She wrote in detail of her pain and agony with her choice of separation. She regretted having let Jenna go. She enclosed photos of herself and Jenna's two older sisters. It took my breath away to see the resemblance between Jenna and one of her sisters. I felt sad for the birth mom, understanding some of the pain she must still be feeling. There was much unresolved grief in this woman's life and ours too.

I called Family Services for counsel on how to tell Jenna about the letter. They advised that I make copies of all the photos and the letter, saying many children react angrily and tear up the letter and pictures. I went to make copies, feeling like I was working undercover, sneaking around!

We told Jenna we had the letter. At first she didn't even want to read it. Then she looked at it and did what the social worker had said was a possibility. Jenna tore up the letter. She was angry, "I don't want anything to do with her!" Jenna was overcome with strong feelings she could not even identify and everything came out as anger.

I was so sad, about all that was happening with my children. I had to let time settle both Jenna and my emotions.

After a time, I asked Jenna if I could respond to her birth mother's letter. Jenna agreed. I wrote about Jenna's life including photos of Jenna at different ages with our family.

Then we got a phone call from Jenna's brother-in-law who was an American soldier who was married to Jenna's sister and living in the USA. He asked if we were "the Jones family" who had adopted his wife's sister. She wanted to talk to Jenna, but Jenna did not want any contact with her sister.

There was no response following the letter to Jenna's mother, until four years later when Jenna was about seventeen. At that time the birth mom asked for an update on Jenna. Jenna still declined any personal response, but she said I could respond again to this letter.

One of my first mission trips was to Sri Lanka and India. I made several contacts and had sent small financial support since then. During this same time our contact in India wrote asking me to please consider adopting a child from his orphanage. He had a small orphanage of fifty kids, a medical clinic and about forty pastors who worked with him evangelizing the surrounding villages. The Indian pastor knew our children were adopted.

Todd was eight years old at the time. I embraced the idea thinking back to our original plan for six children! Terry was hesitant and said he'd pray about it. After some time, he concluded, "I just couldn't get a clear answer, so we can't proceed. We cannot take this child into our family now. But we can continue to send support to help with her care."

I was sad but knew both partners needed to want the child and be in agreement for the blessing to be there. I had to lay down my plan and say, "Yes, Lord. Not my way but yours."

A friend told me when hearing of my grief, "This sounds like a spiritual miscarriage." With those words I could accept the decision as the Lord's will for our family.

Little did I realize what was ahead of us! How God protected us! Now in retrospect, I think, "Josie. Get real! How much more tension did you need in your life?" I was so grateful Terry had stood strong and said no to me. God knew we did not have the strength or fortitude to bring in another child. God knew what lay ahead and that we would be consumed with the cares of those we already had in our home.

Within three months of this decision, we found out Mandy was pregnant and we began a long journey with her and our first grandchild.

9

Mission to Mexico

I am forever grateful that God doesn't require that we "have our act together" before He can use us for kingdom purposes. My first thoughts of going somewhere with the gospel came when we attended a family bible camp. We began to hear wonderful stories of "ordinary people" traveling to Mexico and other countries, bringing Bibles and teaching others about Jesus' love. My previous understanding was that you needed a bible college degree, or had to be a "clergy" person with a religious vocation to go places as a missionary.

We learned families could go to Mexico on a two week trip inexpensively to hand out free Bibles door-to-door. That was a possibility for us! In the fall, I packed up Chad, Jenna and Todd and headed to Monterey Mexico with a group of fifty other Christian people on an old school bus. We ate meals we had prepared and frozen ahead of time, things like sloppy joes, chili, tacos, and lots of PBJ sandwiches. We slept on church floors or in really cheap motels, making the fifteen hundred mile trip in three days.

The leader had seven children. He and his wife believed in bringing the entire family. We had so much fun on the bus ride down to Mexico, singing, telling jokes, and laughing together as the hours rolled on. By the time we arrived we all knew each other well. Our kids became friends on the bus, and we were one big family. It was a great way for the team to bond before the work began. We distributed Bibles door-to-door, showed the *Jesus Film* in neighborhoods, and encouraged the Mexican Christians. We also brought clothing to distribute to the poor.

A couple months after our first trip to Mexico, we left for another mission trip there. This time I took four of our kids: Mandy 17, Chad 14, Jenna 12 and Todd 7. A prevailing memory from this mission trip is the comment of another team member who had seen Mandy feigning sickness and pretending to faint so she could return to the base to avoid the door-to-door work. She was not interested in relating to the Mexican people. She liked the travel experience but not the mission encounters. It was difficult for me to hear this from others perspective.

On our third family journey to Mexico, I convinced Terry to join us. He previously stated emphatically he would *never ride 24 hours on a school bus*. Later he said he enjoyed just riding and not being responsible for the driving. Three of our children came along this time, Chad 16, Jenna 14 and Todd 9.

We went door-to-door paired with the local Mexican Christians who worked very eagerly to share the gospel with their neighbors. We often slaughtered the language as we greeted the people at their doors, "Somos christianos de los Estados Unidos". The people stood in their doorways smiling at us. We were so surprised by their warm welcome often inviting us into their homes for some refreshments. They would send someone out to the store to buy pop or chips immediately. It was so humbling, and very sweet. We felt totally pampered by this. If we said we liked a picture on the wall, they immediately would go to take it off the wall to give us. I still have an afghan given to me as a gift by a lady we visited. Our friendly precocious son Todd, then six, had a huge "stash" of gifts given him by the locals!

I came home from Mexico committed to tell the world about Jesus because I saw firsthand that many didn't know Him. I realized I didn't need a bible school degree to be a messenger for Him. The trips were grueling, often in very warm weather, with no air-conditioned facilities. But I had never felt greater joy then when we were sharing Jesus' love with the Mexican people.

I have two outstanding memories from these trips. The first happened late one evening when we were showing the Jesus film up in the mountain barrios (neighborhoods) around Monterrey. We hung a sheet over the side of the bus and set up the 16MM projector to show the Jesus Film. It was a warm, summer night after sunset with millions of stars glittering brightly across the sky. A crowd of villagers had gathered to watch the film. There was an air of excitement among the people. I warned my kids to stay close to us, because we were in such a large crowd in unknown territory and I didn't want them endangered. The men had to stop in the middle of the film to change reels. While the people waited for the movie to start again our leader took the microphone. People had come to tell what had happened to them as they watched the film. Wanting everyone to hear what they were saying, our leader had the people line up to use the microphone to tell what had happened as they watched the Jesus film! Headaches, backaches, joint pain, crippling had left their bodies! Such is the POWER of Jesus Christ. Those testimonies made me a firm supporter of the Jesus Film Project! I also witnessed the same healings occur in India as people watched and listened to the events of Jesus' life on the movie screen.

My second power-filled memory from Mexico was when we went door-to-door with Bibles. We came upon a man in his front yard working underneath his car. We walked over and yelled to him, as he lay under the car. "We have come with a free gift of a Bible for you."

He politely got out, hands all greasy, and listened intently. We went on to explain, "You must be born again to enter and to understand God's kingdom."

He explained, "I am a Catholic."

"That is good," we went on to explain, "but you still need to personally accept what Jesus did for you on the cross. Jesus provided a sacrifice for your sins."

Under the burning Mexican sun, the hot and sweating man immediately humbly bowed his head, folded his greasy hands, and prayed with tears running down his cheeks. He thanked Jesus for dying for him and asked Jesus to be his Lord and Savior!

I pondered as to whether or not anyone in America would stop what they were doing, and so humbly and intently listen to what strangers were saying about Jesus and respond to The Gospel as this man had. It was a divine moment for him and for me. We were not a bother or interruption to him; but he received us as God's messengers to his life. I was truly experiencing firsthand the words our Lord spoke.

> "The harvest is plentiful but the workers are few. Ask the Lord of the harvest therefore, to send out workers into His harvest field."
> Matthew 9:37-38

After three trips to Mexico, I was given the opportunity to go to India with some ladies from Women Aglow International. Terry agreed I could go and he'd care for our family. I was ecstatic, as I already had previously established contacts in India. I had a pen pal to whom we had sent small donations and we also had been sponsoring a little girl we thought was orphaned. Now I would be able to meet them both face-to-face!

Josie began going on mission trips to foreign lands when the children were 20, 18, 13, 8 and 6. She went about once a year. When I started writing the stories of this family I wondered if perhaps she had unconsciously determined that as a strong Christian woman, knowing she was called to share her faith she was called to the fields that were "white unto harvest." In spite of the family challenges, she heeded a call to go to people ready and willing to listen and receive what she had to offer. Josie had a strong call of service for the Lord and needed to share what she knew about a living Lord Jesus Christ who offered hope and peace to those hungry and needy. The struggles and frustrations within the family may have felt overwhelming at times. The journeys off to faraway places with strange sounding names to meet those willing and eager to listen has provided Josie with a time of refocusing and a renewal of energy to continue her journey at home.

Terry also went to international places of service during these times. He took the older boys individually with him to China, and he went to Costa Rica on a building project.

10

First Search for Birth Parents

We were introduced to the reality of the adoptive family being a triad consisting of the child, the birth parents, and the adoptive parents at our initial adoption meeting.

"Well," I thought, "Okay. So what? Big deal. We know there are birth parents, but we are the ones that will be parenting this child."

We didn't feel any need for *birth parents* in our family during the early years as parents; however, through the years we understood that our children needed to know more about themselves as they began to form their own unique identities. My idealistic perception was that reunion with the birth parents would be a good experience and could be a healthy part of the child's maturation. Later I realized my own personal paradigm for the process of assimilating birth parents into an adopted child's life was far too simplistic. Each adoptee must process the information and the people independently and in their own unique manner. Each reunion experience is unique. There should be no expectations as to what will happen or how the reunion will affect any member of the triad.

As the individuals of the triad come into contact with one another the preconceived fantasies about what had occurred in the past must be replaced with truth. An adopted child often makes up a fantasy about how and why their parent or parents gave them away. The parents who had given the child up for adoption have perhaps fantasized about the "perfect" child they have missed knowing. The adoptive parents have often harshly judged the birth parents and their decision. The previous ideas and fantasies must be replaced with truth as it unfolds. The peace that comes with truth leads to a new freedom of knowing, which alleviates the frustrations of questions unanswered. The connection may lead in many different directions. There should be no expectation of the outcome, for only God knows what will happen as He alone knows all the members of the triad.

Our oldest son Jason was our pioneer in meeting birth parents, as he had been in so many other things. Pioneering comes with the territory of being a first-born. In December of his first year away at college, Jason called to say he had contacted the adoption agency to ask about finding his birth parents. I was totally shocked. I was bewildered and scared. I didn't oppose his search. Both Terry and I had completely forgotten or blocked out of our minds that Jason had told us in counseling, when he was 17 that he wanted to find his birth mother!

(This fact is a glaring example of how our memories are ours alone, and MAY NOT be the same as another's memory of the same moment. It was only in editing the book that we cleared this hurt up with Jason. It is good for families to revisit their past hurts and work through things as best as possible for both parties.)

I was shocked and hurt that Jason wanted to search for his birth mother because I recalled him saying many times that he had no need to find his birth mother because we were his parents. Now he was out of our home only three months and he was searching.

Jason called within a week to tell us the social worker located his parents.

I said, "Parents?"

"Yes. They married each other after they placed me."

This stunned me, to think Jason had found both of his parents. Jason was whirling and buzzing with excitement. They exchanged letters first, and then arranged to meet at the agency. Jason had several meetings with them and returned happy and then wanted us to meet them. It was all happening so fast. We arranged to meet at a restaurant, per our social worker's advice. She had told us it was a safe place, where either party could easily exit if things were uncomfortable. By this time the birth parents had already given Jason a check for $5000 for his education, and made arrangements for him to meet his birth half-sister.

Terry wondered if this generous gift was to buy their son's affection and an attempt to become his "real parents." I, too, was scared they were trying to woo him away from us. I watched Jason walk through this maze of meeting his birth family, and deciding what type of relationship he wanted to have with them. I learned an adoption search could be a minefield for any member of the triad: child, birthparents and adoptive parents. I definitely believe the energy expended in contacting the birth parents is worth the investment to identify truth in one's life.

We walked into the restaurant and there stood this handsome couple waiting to greet us. Jason's birth dad was very tall, outgoing and gregarious. His mother was very gracious and attractive but much more reserved. As I sat across the booth from them I was amazed how many similarities I could notice between my son and these two strangers. Jason has his mother's penetrating steel blue eyes, his father's same hand gestures, his father's same smile, his mother's same intelligent perceptive manner. Jason is confident like his father, almost to the point of being arrogant at times. Jason had received his good looks from both parents.

I was tense and filled with anxiety but also excited. In some ways it felt surreal. Here we were, all four of us connected so deeply, and yet having no history together, but linked together in a very intimate way for life by decisions we all made nineteen years earlier.

Jason's birthparents told him their story of how they had married each other nine months after placing him. They had met at the office. The birth father was married and the father of five children. The birth mother was divorced and had one daughter five years older than Jason. Jason began his journey to get to know his siblings, with the same gusto he took on most things in life! He heard some stories that sent him home to us in tears. This time was emotionally hard for him and hard for us as he began telling us what was happening as he met the two full families of stepsiblings. He was invited to a stepsibling's graduation party. The birth parents told their other children about him, after their meeting with Jason. Eventually things calmed down.

One reunion experience of an adoptive situation is like another reunion experience only to the extent that truth is found about the beginnings. Other than that each experience will be unique. Some of the questions and ponderings of the hearts may be quieted by addressing these questions but there is no guarantee regarding the outcome of such an experience of meeting birth parents.

I remember vividly my first Mother's Day after Jason found his birthparents. I was asking the Lord to comfort me about my fears of emotionally losing Jason.

God spoke to me very clearly through these words in John, I was not to worry about my relationship with Jason. God was telling me Jason and I were solid, that Jason loved me as his mom!

> "When Jesus saw His mother standing there, and the disciple whom He loved standing nearby, He said to His mother, Dear woman here is your son, and to the disciple, here is your mother." John 19:26-27a

After church that day, Jason left on his motorcycle for a while. He came back about two and one half-hours later. I was like a "cat" pacing the house, wondering where he went. Did he drive to the north suburbs to see "her"? When he came in I asked him where he had been! It must have been written all over my face because he grinned and said, "Don't worry mom, I didn't go to see her. You're my mom and always will be!"

I went up to my bedroom and cried. Those words from Jason settled my heart down, and I can honestly say it relieved me of fear that we would "lose him" to the birth family. Our family had so many conflicts going on that I thought Jason would possibly want to walk away to a more "ideal" life.

Jason asked if his birth parents could be in the second row, behind us, at his wedding a year later. We assured him it was fine. But when we saw his birth family at the motel swimming pool, prior to the ceremony, I confess I felt jealous of them. After the wedding when they posed for pictures with Jason and Karla I had to just look away. They were such a handsome couple, and looked way more sophisticated than us; my own self-esteem was definitely in question.

Basically, I must admit my feelings in the search for birth parents experiences are that I really did not want to share my kids with anyone. I wanted them to be "mine" alone. This separateness could never be, for it was not truth. Our adopted children were a blend of their genetic birthparents and their time living with us. We were connected whether I wanted something different or not.

11

Mandy Parenting

As high school graduation approached Mandy had been in and out of our home, home schooled, and attended the public high school. Graduation was uncertain until the last days when she found out she had enough credits to graduate. We had an open house to celebrate!

Mandy had an apartment, a roommate and enough money for three months' rent when she left our home one month before her eighteenth birthday.

Mandy was 19 when her first child, a daughter, Tyesha was born. Krista, our foster daughter, was Mandy's labor coach. Krista and I were at the hospital, together with Peanut the father of Mandy's baby. Peanut, a tall, skinny, cocky Afro-American man was very talkative that day, probably high on some drug! He stood at the foot of her bed saying "The Our Father" and also quoting Bible verses at her at very inappropriate times as she struggled in her labor. It was unnerving for me to say the least! I felt like I would go crazy with the incongruities in his behavior.

After Tyesha's birth I walked out of the hospital with Peanut. He announced, "We are going home to make more babies and fill the phone book with the William's name!" (Unfortunately he now has six more children by three other women. It is very frustrating to me that our tax dollars go to pay for children because their fathers "skip out" on their responsibility. I would like to see stricter consequences for failure to pay child support.)

Mandy, Tyesha and Peanut went home to their apartment. When we did get to see our grandchild, Tyesha, we could tell her care was questionable. She had severe cradle cap. When we would pick Mandy and the baby up for a visit, there were dirty diapers everywhere on the floor. Tyesha never got her regular baby shots or checkups. Several times we had Mandy stay overnight at our home with Tyesha. I'd have to shake Mandy awake during the night to take care of her crying child. This meant to me that she didn't hear her at home either. Finally, I just fed the baby. Tyesha would be in dirty clothes that were too big or torn. We knew Mandy owned nicer baby clothes but she had no idea where they were.

We tried to let Peanut, Mandy and Tyesha live their lives. Sometimes Mandy would call for help, saying Peanut was being abusive. We talked and talked to Mandy about leaving him, but she refused to do it. During this time I called the County Child Protection Unit to report our concerns. This was humbling, to say the least, since I myself had been a child protection worker years earlier. Child Protection would not take action.

All during this time I would be crying out to the Lord for wisdom. Terry and I often felt we were trying to save a sinking ship, by bailing out thimblefuls of water. We were concerned when we didn't see Mandy and the baby for long periods of time but more worried after we saw them! The Psalms were a constant source of strength and comfort to my heart. God would always give a word of encouragement as I read each morning.

> "When anxiety was great with me Your consolation brought joy to my soul." Psalm 94:19
>
> "Cast your cares on the Lord and He will sustain you; He will never let the righteous fall." Psalm 55:22

My mother's heart felt heavy like we were walking in a dark tunnel. Mandy was not taking good care of herself or her daughter and she was not changing. She was not hearing or taking the suggestions to help her do a better job parenting.

Mandy called us one time and said she and Peanut had been evicted and they had to find a place to live. She asked if we would take care of the baby. We took the baby, both because we felt a need to protect her, and also because we enjoyed our first grandchild. After *two weeks*, I called Mandy asking her to set a time to give Tyesha back. Mandy protested, saying they had no place to take Tyesha. Again I called the county about the situation, and they said the threat to the baby's safety was not serious enough for them to get involved.

Eventually, Mandy said they were going to live with Peanut's aunt for a while so I was to return the baby to them. At the time I was driving across a bridge to the city returning Tyesha to her two immature young parents. I heard the Lord say, "This will all work out peacefully."

I remember crying out to God, "*How* can this end peacefully?" This memory is very significant. I had a strong impression that the Lord responded to my heart, "This *will* work out peacefully." I am still waiting...

Mandy and Peanut stood on a street corner. When I drove up, I handed four-month-old Tyesha over to them, and drove away! It ripped my heart out to think of what type of care she would get. I had to trust the words the Lord had spoken to me. The three of them lived with his relatives off and on for a few months. Mandy's attitude was never one of fear or desperation, but always confident that things would be better tomorrow. We contacted County Child Protection again, and finally a social worker was assigned to the case.

We were desperate for Mandy to grow up now that she was a mother.

Mandy called one day to say she and eleven month old Tyesha had been living in a shelter but were now in a motel. Mandy did not appear to be one bit emotionally upset about living in a motel, but acted quite cheerful. She reported they had no food. I drove over and took her to the grocery store to get bread, milk, peanut butter, and crackers. I begged her to leave Peanut!

Her response was, "I'll handle this by myself."

Mandy and Peanut announced that summer they were pregnant again. Peanut was getting his wish of filling a phone book with his offspring, much to our dismay. I emphatically explained to Mandy that if she wanted help with Tyesha while delivering the new baby, she needed to make arrangements with us ahead of time. She needed to officially ask us, and make a plan. Mandy agreed, "Sure. We can do that."

She did not make arrangements.

Then the call came from Peanut asking us to come quickly to take Tyesha because Mandy was ready to go to the hospital to have her baby.

This was another one of those "tough love" decisions we had to make with Mandy. We said, "No." We could not do what she was asking as she had not made the prior arrangements we had agreed upon. I felt awful about this, but knew I needed to trust God with this baby, if we ever wanted Mandy to become accountable for herself and her family.

Tyesha wound up staying with Mandy's best friend Tehanna in her apartment.

It turned out to be the right decision for us to make, because now Tehanna saw the lack of care, and became involved in getting help for Tyesha. Tehanna was very angry because Peanut and Mandy brought Tyesha to her with no diapers, formula, or clothes. Tehanna then understood and became our ally in securing help for the children from the county.

Jewel was born fourteen months after Tyesha. She was an adorable little baby, with a head full of very curly black hair. Peanut and Mandy brought the baby home to their downtown apartment.

This part of the story is fuzzy to me. I think I was so stressed that I can't recall the exact details; but, for some reason we had been keeping Mandy and Peanut's girls at our home. Maybe Mandy was looking for work or a place to live or something. One week turned into two weeks, and then three weeks. We got very tired of all her excuses about why she wasn't coming for the girls. I called Mandy on a Tuesday and told her she needed to pick up her children by noon on Thursday or we were going to take them to St. Angelina's Children's Home and declare them abandoned. We had been advised to do this by the county social worker in order to engage outside intervention.

Thursday noon came and went. We packed up the few clothes the girls came with, and headed to St. Angelina's. We kept the clothes we had purchased for them. We explained to the girls what might happen, as much as they could understand. We told them we may not see them for a few days but we surely would see them as soon as we could. The intake worker interviewed us, as the social worker had called ahead, and alerted them of our situation. We were just finishing, about 1:30 when in the door walked Mandy. She started protesting, saying she wanted her children back. The intake people took her in a room and interviewed her. We were advised to leave, and told we would be notified. Later we got a call that indeed the girls were going into an

Afro-American foster home, and that child protection was going to work with Mandy.

Leaving the girls behind was so hard and sad, but we knew we had to get help from the authorities. This procedure was what we had been advised to do. We had to put our own feelings aside to think of the girls' over-all welfare. We were desperate to get Mandy to face her life. We knew our caring for her children enabled her life of irresponsibility.

My sustaining strength always came from the Lord and His word. I had been to Israel on a mission trip, and visited Jerusalem. Mountains surround the city of Jerusalem, and the highway winds up the mountain slowly to reach the city at the top. It seems so protected by God! I could shut my eyes and envision the Lord's care all around us in these troubled waters. God was telling me to hang on and trust Him, and He would work things out hour by hour.

"Those who trust in the Lord are like Mount Zion, which cannot be shaken, but endures forever. As the mountains surround Jerusalem, so the Lord surrounds His people, both now and forevermore."
Psalm 125:1-2

My biggest challenge was to live in the present, not worrying about the future or what or when the next crisis would be.

Mandy was free to pursue her life of irresponsibility with the girls in foster care. Soon Peanut was arrested for the attempted murder of Mandy. The police report states that Peanut shot at Mandy's head as she was running from the apartment. A witness called the police so it was a citizen's arrest. Mandy refused to file charges against Peanut, but the police arrested him based on the witness' report. God had protected our daughter again. Only heaven knows how many other times God spared her life. Remember He told me, "My eye is on the sparrow."

Mandy told us, "He didn't really mean it! He was just kidding. He wouldn't hurt me."

I believe it was all a part of a drunken stupor on both their parts. I actually saw the incident as an answered prayer. Mandy did not get hurt, and it forced Peanut into prison, away from our daughter! Three months before it happened I had been praying this scripture for Mandy:

> "Break the arm of the wicked and evil man;
> call him to account for his wickedness that
> would not be found out." Psalm 10:15

The girls were placed in an Afro-American foster home. We were given visitation rights at our home, every other weekend. Mandy had the same privilege. The girls lived in the foster home for one year and Mandy never even went to see them. On our weekend visits, we gave time and attention to the girls, nurturing them with the safety and security of family, in an attempt to continue maintaining family ties. We hoped Mandy would wake up and realize the wonderful gifts the girls were for her. We lived in a mindset of minimizing what had already occurred in the girls' lives, denying the damages of those events and wishful thinking for the future. We loved the girls and enjoyed our weekends with them.

We loved the foster mom and were grateful to her for opening her home to our grandchildren. The agency policy at that time specified biracial children had to go to a black foster home. I challenged the county social worker that the girls were also half white, and I saw no reason to discriminate against a white foster home. There was no discussion on the matter, only a black home would be considered.

Loretta was an awesome foster mom. She was a heavy, buxom woman who was confident, nurturing and calm. Loretta had fostered many children, and seemed comfortable with chaos. Our granddaughter, little baby Jewel, lay up on her bosom as content as could be. Several strangers were always in the room when we came to pick up the girls, and we were never introduced to anyone. The TV was always on at full volume. The girls were always clean, well fed, and seemed very happy in Loretta's home. They thrived on a regular schedule. Loretta had four other foster kids, and her own three children.

Loretta told the social worker that Tyesha frequently tried to "hump" the other children, and the toys. I didn't even know what the word meant, until the worker gave me an explanation that this was about simulating sex. Loretta began working with Tyesha on these behaviors, teaching Tyesha right from wrong.

Loretta introduced us to different cultural mores concerning childcare. Childcare was *ok* if anyone in the family bloodline cared for the children: Aunt, Uncle, or other relatives. Having others raise your children was acceptable. Loretta saw this process as "letting the parents grow up a little" before they faced the total responsibility of their own children.

Loretta announced she was going to potty train Tyesha, now twenty months old, "this weekend." I laughed and asked how she was going to do that. She said she would only concentrate on Tyesha all weekend, watching her and offering her the pot, wearing no diapers that weekend! I thought to myself, "Sure you will!" Sure enough the next weekend when we picked the girls up, Tyesha was potty trained. I was impressed. Loretta ran a loving, loose, nurturing ship. Besides all that, she was a Christian, attending church weekly.

Our hearts ached having our first grandchildren in foster care, but we felt it had been directed by the Lord, in an effort to awaken Mandy.

Our pastor had told us that if we took the girls, long term, we were telling Mandy to go have more children and we would continue to take care of them. No way did we want to send that message!

One year went by with the girls visiting us every other weekend in our home. I became frustrated because nothing was changing. Finally I called the social worker and asked what the plan was. Her response was, "Oh, we should be holding Mandy accountable".

The county kicked in, contacted Mandy, and directed her into an alcohol and drug treatment program for thirty days. She had to comply in order to regain custody of her children. After completing the thirty days, she was sent to a transitional home for moms with young children. The program seemed like a perfect program, because they would help her with parenting issues, while she lived in their center. Mandy thrived there, as she always did, with structure and rules. She could function very well, when someone else was setting boundaries for her and holding her accountable.

First Tyesha went back to live with Mandy, while Jewel came to our home during a trial period for evaluating how Mandy could handle one child. Eventually Mandy brought Jewel home, also. We were glad, hoping and believing this was the change in Mandy's life. Mandy graduated from the parenting program in 3 months' time and moved into her own place.

Mandy did well for about three weeks. Then the girls mentioned a guy named Damien to us. We found him hiding behind the door when we came to visit one evening! We later discovered he was "the man from Hell."

I was in prayer one day when I got an idea of how to demonstrate to Mandy what was happening in her life. I felt impressed to wrap a piece of coal in a box, and to put a beautiful diamond ring (fake zirconium) in another box. I brought these two gifts to Mandy and asked her to open them, the "black" box first. She looked sufficiently puzzled and I explained that this might be how she saw herself, *but* God and we saw her differently. Then she opened the "diamond" box, and grinned. I explained that this was how God saw her, and He valued her a lot. She smiled and thanked me. I never did hear how this affected her, if at all.

Rarely if ever, was Mandy rude or unkind to me personally. Although she listened to our suggestions, Mandy would go on with her life and nothing changed. Mandy participated in the conversation, verbally agreed with suggestions, but did nothing. An example would be taking her girls in to get immunizations. She would agree, but never do it. I was totally frustrated with her inconsistencies. I thought she was deliberately lying.

The girls were now three and a half, and four and a half.

All the other children in the family were aware of Mandy's behavior. The parental focus and anxiety was part of their everyday life during these times. The traumatic consequences for each individual were probably not apparent while they were living in the chaos.

Chad was old enough to understand the abuse and neglect relating to the hard decisions that the parents made regarding the care of the granddaughters. Jenna may have been escaping, when at this time she left the home for her mission with Teen Mania. Todd was observing but perhaps not understanding about what was happening without even knowing how to ask about the dilemma with the grandchildren and Mandy. All their lives must have been chaotic.

This is a family. All the children are in relationship with all the others. When the "squeaky wheel gets the grease" or the child in *conflict demands all the energy and attention of the parents, the others often feel pushed aside and also threatened with the parental decisions. The intense parental concern and focus for one child in crisis can jeopardize the other children and leave them in a place of emotional neglect. When choices of placement in other facilities with other caregivers occur, each child may feel threatened and fear abandonment if they do not comply with the parental expectations. Each child will have their own interpretations of what they observe, and may not be able to voice their understanding and their concern with the parents. **Communication** is the most important part with each and every member of the family and may help alleviate the unspoken fears and misunderstandings.*

Mandy got a job at the video store across the street from where she lived. Sometimes when Mandy came to visit us we noticed bruises on her face. She of course denied they were from her current live-in boyfriend, Damien. We stayed clear of her place, because we were afraid of Damien. The girls still came over for visits. They started telling us stories about how Damien disciplined them when Mandy worked. They also told us Damien had a gun, which Mandy confirmed offhandedly, "Sure many people living in the city do."

The girls told some gruesome stories about how they had been disciplined. They had to hold pennies to the wall with their forehead and were locked in the basement. They told us about their mom asking them to get her a cigarette while she and Damien were in bed naked. Damien would have them watch dirty movies with him. Terry was suspicious that these explicit sexual situations were part of a plan Damien had to prepare the girls for child prostitution.

Again our anxiety about these events motivated us to call Child Protection. We shared all the information we had but the official response was that the case wasn't serious enough to warrant intervention; no blood or broken bones.

The thing that seemed to disturb the girls the most was the threat that "sweaty man" would come and get them. Both girls told us their mom threatened them that there was a man outside their bedroom window, and if they didn't obey, he would grab them. They always had to have the shades drawn in a room because of their fear. They both had terrifying nightmares about the "sweaty man" and would wake up screaming. We prayed with them for peace, and assured them they were safe with us. We confronted Mandy and the look on her face indicated she was totally unconcerned and our accusations were not true. Mandy would respond to our accusations, "Mom! You know those girls lie about everything. They make up stories. They have vivid imaginations!"

On one visit Tyesha came with belt marks on her back, and rib cage. The girls told us Damien had used the belt. We called our local police for advice. An officer came to our home and took photos for the records. The police indicated the girls were from another county and that is where the reports should be filed, our county could do nothing. (We used all this evidence later when we filed a civil law suit seeking custody of the girls.)

When we asked Mandy about it she minimized it, saying, "Tyesha had misbehaved. The girls were playing with a toy telephone and marks were from the telephone cord." We were beside ourselves with worry, but again, the Lord would comfort us. We kept asking Him to intervene here, (as He had done with Peanut's arrest and imprisonment.) Again we prayed:

> "Break the arm of the wicked and evil man;
> call him to account for his wickedness that
> would not be found out." Psalm 10:15

83

The stormy relationship between Mandy and Damien lasted almost two years. In the fall, we met Mandy at a restaurant to talk about the sexual abuse the girls had mentioned to us. We told her about Damien forcing them to watch dirty movies when she was at work. Her response was to get up and run out of the restaurant, saying, "The police are probably coming to get me!"

During this time we became really concerned, to the point of panicking, because we could see Todd was slipping into depression. He started to become very rebellious toward us, spending most of his time in his room or out of the house with friends. He agreed to go to counseling, so we sought a psychologist with good recommendations.

The psychologist gave Todd a TOVA test; an indicator of ability to stay focused, and concluded that Todd was ADD and also suffering from depression. The psychologist stated Todd was burdened emotionally with the problems of some of his friends and older siblings. He was able to tell us what was happening with his friends. We shared his grave concern for his friends but Todd wasn't willing to bring them to our church youth group. I wanted them to hear about God's great love for them. We insisted Todd go to youth group; in retrospect, we probably should have given him a choice.

At that time, in the midst of all our cares and struggles of beginning to seek court action to gain custody of Mandy's girls, Jenna seemed to be angry about most everything. Jenna seemed mad at the world all the time. One morning she woke up and went out on the screen porch and screamed, "Shut up you birds!" It was a beautiful sunny summer morning, but she woke up angry at the birds that were making too much noise! She was one angry girl. She acted like she had emotional menstrual upset almost every day. She was not rebellious about rules or family decisions, but just angry, so very angry at the world in general.

Jenna had loved our mission trips and became involved in teen ministry trips on her own for two years. She earned her own financing by baking and selling loaves of bread. She sold her bread at Terry's office and around the neighborhood. Jenna worked diligently to gather funds for her mission work ahead.

Repeatedly we spoke to Mandy about leaving Damien, but she refused to do anything to protect herself or her daughters.

One summer evening the phone rang and it was Mandy saying, "Damien is beating me! Please call 911."

We did. We called back minutes later to check and a policeman answered the phone. I told him, "I am Mandy's mother. I called 911 for her."

The Officer said, "They're both nuts! They both belong in jail for beating each other."

I pleaded with him, "Officer, please help us and DO IT."

Mandy called a little later to say they took Damien to jail. We drove over to talk to her, and see if she was all right. When we walked in she was all excited, blood running down her leg. She had a ready excuse, "Oh that must have happened when I kicked my leg through his car window!"

The girls came running out of the bedroom with only under shirts on. They reported, "Grandma, we prayed for God to help us!"

We asked Mandy to come to our house for the night with the girls, to get some rest in a safe place. She wanted to stay home and guard her stereo. Mandy was afraid Damien's friends would come in and steal her stereo if she left their apartment vacant!

Finally, she agreed to come home with us. We bathed the girls and put them to bed. They were three and four at this time. Mandy and I sat on the porch talking. I asked her, "Why do you live like this? Why do you let yourself be treated like this?"

I shared our fear for her and the girls. She had no answer, but said she was going to do something "this time." We went to bed at about 12:30 a.m.

I awoke the next morning to a note, "Mom, sorry, I had to go home and protect my stuff." I was furious, frightened, and very emotionally discouraged. Terry and I decided we had to do something to protect our granddaughters.

We contacted a family attorney to pursue custody through the civil court.

12

Residual Pain

I vividly recall when seventeen-year-old Chad came to us one Saturday night. He had been out with friends and returned about eleven PM. He normally did return at or before curfew, which thrilled us.

I usually waited up for the kids but Terry was up this night too. Chad came in and sat on the sofa and visited for a while. It was one of those rare times when Chad shared his thoughts and feelings. I call those "serendipity" moments, but I believe they are God ordained.

Chad initiated a very unusual conversation with us. Chad asked Terry and I both to pray for him that he would not carry on any of the sins of his biological father. Chad said he didn't know what these were, but must have had some thoughts about it. We asked, "What are you thinking?"

Chad said, "I have heard so many stories about adopted kids and all their troubles, so I think I should pray so it doesn't have to happen to me. I don't want to be a problem to you." We knew from Chad's birth records that his mom left her husband when pregnant with Chad, because she wanted to get away from the father, and felt she couldn't support two children. Chad was the second born child. Chad said he wanted to lead a good, moral life, and he knew he needed God's help to be the person he wanted to be. I wept for his tenderness, and gladly agreed to pray with and for him, for breaking of any generational curses that would keep him from being all God wanted him to be, and that he would experience God's best in his life.

[Generational curses are behavior or thinking patterns that families promote or pass on from one generation to the next. These practices can only be changed or broken if we purposely choose new ways of thinking and behaving, based on truth and God's Word, as I said earlier. There was a family sin or curse of lust in my family of origin. My mother loved to tell off-colored stories, gathering jokes and encouraging them to be repeated in our home. I was NOT about to repeat this in my own life or with our children. I asked the Lord's forgiveness and purposed to speak wholesome words in our home. Purity was a value I wanted for myself and my home. I had to go against my family system and I received much teasing for my ways. I wanted to honor God in all areas of my life. Fear is another trait that is easily passed down in families, fear of failure, fear of success, fear of man. I came from a long line of people afraid of what others would think! Generational blessings are also passed down this way. My father was extremely generous to the poor; it is a deep value of mine also!]

Chad had probably been thinking of Mandy and her situation. The entire family had been dealing with her painful choices.

Chad's plan after he graduated was to work full time, and live at home, without paying room and board. We believed that our children should be contributing members of the household after age eighteen, if they were working and not attending school. Chad was very angry with this, so we sought a counselor to help us find some compromise solution. Terry wanted Chad to attend at least one year of Bible College, to establish the tenants of our faith in his heart. Our compliant son Chad agreed to this, since we paid for half his tuition. Chad hated the school and hated us for "imposing" this on him. At least that is how he interpreted it. Chad still holds resentment towards us, even though we have both asked forgiveness several times.

During this time Chad started to use marijuana regularly. When we learned about this, we refused to pay for another semester of school. Chad left and went to another city where his high school friends were attending school. He roomed with them for several years. The only time we heard from him was when we contacted him. We were very sad at his distancing from us and we felt rejected by Chad.

At the same time, we had Todd in counseling for depression. By thirteen Todd's anger began to escalate. The more we asked questions or pried the angrier he became. Our youth pastor had asked for a meeting with Todd and us in his office. The pastor had been concerned about Todd's behavior in youth group and wanted to confront him with us there. The very day of our appointment at church one of Todd's friends called advising me to ask Todd to pull up his shirtsleeves. Our Pastor spoke kindly to Todd about the youth group's desire to draw Todd in to closer fellowship with them. Todd sat there sullen, and unresponsive.

As his friend had suggested, I asked Todd to please pull up his shirtsleeve for us. He looked at me with great hesitation in his eyes. I honestly had no clue why the friend had asked us to confront Todd in this way. I was a naïve parent who had no idea what other kids were doing. Todd's arms were covered with many wounds, some cuts deeper than others. He had been cutting (self-mutilating) himself. His arm was wounded and raw with self-inflicted marks and scars; clearly showing the amount of pain our son was in. I wanted to faint and scream at the same time. It looked so incredibly painful. I was stunned and baffled as to why anyone would do this. I felt such deep love for my son and such deep pain for him at the same time. Todd said he didn't know why he did it; things just felt better when he did it.

The psychologist Todd had already been seeing for six months told us this behavior was a way to release deep psychic pain; the pain of cutting relieved tension of inner conflicts and gave some catharsis to the pain. We were advised to keep all sharp objects out of his reach, and try to be as gentle, encouraging and reassuring as we possibly could be. We were told the behavior would pass and we were not to focus on it. It took tremendous self-control and grace not to be checking on him all the time. Our psychologist suggested we place Todd on anti-depressants. It took several tries before we found one that seemed to really help him. The behavior did abate, and Todd began engaging in life again. We had our son back, so to speak, but it had been a long three-year journey for Todd while we were trying to help with Mandy's daughters.

One evening the mother of one of Todd's friends called and asked if we could talk. Todd and her daughter had been spending a lot of time together. She explained that their daughter had gone into depression, and that they had put her in the hospital. The mom went on to tell me of her daughter's involvement in witchcraft. She had her room decorated in occult themes, with cobwebs, and black lights. It was then I learned Todd had also been experimenting with witchcraft and reading lots of books about casting curses and spells on people. I explained to this mom that this was very real and a very scary thing for these two to be doing. There were spiritual forces of darkness with real powers that deeply offend God, and causes spiritual consequences on the children. Todd gave us several examples of times they had "cast hexes or curses" on teachers and then would observe things happen to the teachers the same day. We both forbid the kids to read any more books about spells, and the girl was made to dismantle her bedroom décor of the "dark side".

Todd eventually stopped spending time with this group of friends. The use of anti-depression medicines also seemed to level out his behavior and attitudes. I don't know if Todd ever dealt with the spiritual component of being involved with occult activities. Much like sexual abuse, I believe witchcraft affects a person's spirit and they need to actively seek prayer and counseling for healing.

13

Mandy's Birth Mother

A single mother of two daughters, Mandy now twenty-one, decided it was time for her to learn about her own birth parents. Mandy went to the agency and asked for information about her birth parents. Mandy's reunion story had an entirely different twist than Jason's. Her search took much longer than Jason's had because her birth mom re-fused to respond to the social worker. That should have been our first clue. I think Mandy wrote a letter to her first, with no response. The social worker released the file to Mandy who shared with us the information given to the agency at the time of Mandy's birth.

The description of the birthmother was extremely negative. I observed how blunt the social worker was, saying the birth mother had the "lowest self-esteem" she had ever seen! She described an extremely obese unkempt person with poor relational skills.

Mandy set up appointments twice to meet her birth mother Darlene, but Darlene cancelled them. Mandy's information included the place where her mother worked. After the two cancelations, Mandy took matters into her own hands; she took one friend with her and went to the store. She asked at the service counter, "Is Darlene here today?" Mandy was directed to the department where Darlene was working. Mandy walked up to her birth mother Darlene and said, "Hi. I'm your daughter. I hope you're not prejudiced against blacks!"

Mandy reported to us that Darlene was guarded but friendly.

Mandy called me that night to tell me she had gone to the store to meet her birth mom. Mandy told me Darlene cried, but she herself had not cried until she got home. "It did something inside me, I cried all day after meeting her."

Two days later Mandy and I met for breakfast and Mandy was now treating the reunion much more flippantly. She reported that she had thought her birth mother would know her when she walked up to her, but she hadn't. I explained to Mandy that people usually use a counselor to help them do these things; but, since she had already tried to contact Darlene through the agency, to no avail, going by herself indicated her urgency and persistence in her quest to KNOW her birth mother. Mandy said, "She seemed on guard about not keeping me. She told me she would have me come over to her home to meet the rest of the family."

She never heard from Darlene again, but started to relate with a half-sister named Dawn, who lived at home with Darlene. Dawn was two years older than Mandy. They began going "out" to the bars, but soon drifted apart. When Mandy called the house for Dawn, if Darlene answered she would pass the phone to Dawn without even greeting her own daughter.

Mandy reported the phone calls to us. She would laugh and shrug off the pain of this additional repeated rejection, perhaps in an attempt to minimize the pain.

I was searching for answers all the time as to why we were having such a hard time with Mandy. I wanted our love to be enough for her. I often felt desperate to help her settle down, and help her accept that she was lovable. One of my illusions was when Mandy was able to meet her birth mother, her self-esteem issues would be resolved and she would find peace. That didn't happen, as Mandy's birth mom did not want to meet which increased her feelings of rejection and abandonment.

During this time, while visiting Mandy's kids in foster care, Terry and I were preparing for a mission trip to Russia, to distribute Bibles to schools. Our family was also busy working together making a float with an arch of balloons and the slogan, "His Banner Over Me is Love" for the Jesus Parade in our city. The activities of our family life were always multifaceted, each day so busy and full of activities and projects. Now I regret our life was not a little quieter, so we could have had more awareness of what was going on in each of our children's lives. We were always busy with something!

14

Court Intervention

Due to all that had happened with Mandy and her children, we had reached the point where our love and concern for our own daughter Mandy, was not our foremost concern any longer. She was an adult and we couldn't stop the choices she was making for herself. But, where was the line between letting go, tough love, and wisdom for the safety of her innocent children?

Our hearts desire was for Mandy to mature, to grow up, and to want to be a parent, and take the daily concerns and care of her daughters seriously. It wasn't happening. No matter how we prayed, no matter what we said, she chose the men and alcohol in her life over the children.

Terry and I both felt after three years of watching this horror, we had to defend our grandchildren and intervene with the help of the courts. Terry found the name of a good family law attorney as we were considering the idea of a civil law suit to gain custody of our grandchildren. The final fiasco had been Mandy's decision to go back to her home to "protect her furniture" rather than to stay with her girls the day Damien was arrested. This confirmed our need to intervene on the girls' behalf.

Terry and I agreed it was now time we should call the family law attorney to initiate a child protection custody case. We had the assurance that God was on our side. We felt responsible to help these children have a safe environment.

> "Remember the poor and needy, deliver them from the hand of the wicked." Psalm 82:4
>
> "The Lord is close to the brokenhearted and saves those who are crushed in spirit. A righteous man may have many troubles, but the Lord delivers him from them all!" Psalm 34:18-19

We met initially with the family lawyer, Rita Lang, to tell her of our concern and ask her counsel as to whether or not we had a case. We explained our desire to get the girls out of Mandy's control to protect them. We also wanted a psychological exam ordered for our daughter, so we would know what we were dealing with in terms of mental health issues. She told us how to proceed to build a file and how to get police records by ourselves to save legal fees. Rita felt we had more than enough evidence, but warned us that courts generally favored parents.

Our lawyer took four hours of deposition notes at our next meeting. Reliving each situation for the attorney was extremely draining, as the feelings from the events would flood over me again. Rita explained that the more detail we had the more time we would save in court. We were shocked when we saw the police files indicating that the police had been to Mandy's home 22 times in one month. The reports had been filed for various things from domestic abuse to disturbing the peace.

I remember one morning sliding my leg over the side of the bed, feeling tremendous shame thinking of the messes we were being dragged through, and I heard the Lord's voice in my heart say, "Psalm 25". After I got up and read the psalm I cried with thanksgiving to my Father who knew where I was at this time. I am so grateful for His words in Psalm 25.

> "To You oh Lord I lift up my soul; in You I trust oh
> my God. Do not let me be put to *shame*, nor let my
> enemies triumph over me. No one whose hope is in
> You will ever be put to *shame*." Psalm 25:1-3a

The morning of our first hearing I was praying, asking the Lord for peace. He gave me another verse in Psalm 11. We went to court with a little less fear and trepidation.

> "For the Lord is righteous, He loves justice, and
> upright men will see His face." Psalm 11:7

Mandy and Damien were there, sitting down the hall from us. We acknowledged each other. Mandy was smiling and appeared very confident while I was feeling embarrassed to have to be there. Shame was a feeling that would harass me throughout the whole ordeal but Psalm 25 continued to give me comfort.

We had started a court action against our own daughter and were now sitting in the courtroom. My mother's heart felt deep concern for our defenseless grandchildren.

The judge called for order in the court. She asked our attorney to state our request, which was asking for temporary legal custody, beginning immediately. Mandy's attorney, from the county, argued the point and defended Mandy's rights. At one point the judge asked Mandy what she thought. We were seated at a long table, opposite each other: Mandy, Damien, and her lawyer on one side, our attorney and us on the other.

Mandy spoke boldly, "I don't want these people as parents anymore. I want to be free of them. They just cause me trouble."

The Judge replied, "Young lady, from all I read these people have done quite a lot for you, and you should be grateful they are in your life!"

We were given every other weekend visitation with the girls until we returned to court 6 weeks later. The court ordered both parties to meet with a court social worker for evaluation. The court also appointed a guardian ad litem, Mrs. Bench, to represent Tyesha and Jewel. The judge allowed the children to stay with Mandy. The guardian was directed to visit and observe the girls in both homes, and come back with a report. We made a date for Mrs. Bench to come to our home when the girls were visiting. I felt like I was being inspected through a magnifying glass. The guardian wanted all family members living in the household to be present while she was there for the visit. That was Todd (age 13), and Jenna (age 18) at the time.

When Mrs. Bench came for her visit, we played the girls favorite game Memory. We showed her our home and where the girls slept. The two-hour visit felt very uncomfortable. It was worse than the inspection and evaluation when we had applied to adopt our first child. We were willing to endure this intrusion to go through the due process of the law. Mrs. Bench did the same thing with Mandy, Damien, and the girls at Mandy's home.

We made an appointment with the court appointed social worker and had a pleasant interview with him. He asked us for Mandy's current address and phone number to confirm his information. Mandy had disregarded the court ordered evaluation and would not respond to the court social worker. At the next hearing the social worker recommended we be given custody because of Mandy's disregard of the court orders.

The guardian reported that Mandy and Damien were willing to work with a counselor of their choice on family issues and they were willing to cooperate with the court. Mrs. Bench's assessment of Terry and I was that we were "a rich suburbanite family who didn't agree with our daughter's life choices so we were trying to punish her by taking her children away." We were hurt and angry at her judgment of our motives.

The judge sided with the guardian and disregarded the recommendation of the court social worker. We continued to have every-other weekend visitation. Mrs. Bench continued to work as the girls' guardian to look after the girls' interests. We later found out the guardian had over a hundred children to protect and was also paid per child by the court to do these evaluations, this seemed to be an extremely heavy caseload for someone making such life-altering decisions.

Mandy and Damien were directed to find their own social worker that would review the case and send a report to the judge. This process took over a year, and this report, requested by the judge at the very first hearing was the turning point for the custody battle. During that year we still had every other weekend visitation with the girls.

Mandy and Damien were assigned to a social service agency that helps families struggling with multiple issues.

We had several additional court hearings, but the judge always continued the case waiting for the social worker's evaluation of Mandy and Damien.

Mandy, after a year's delay, met with her choice of psychologists who sent an evaluation to the court. Mandy and Damien met several times with Mr. K., the social worker of their choice. He sent his report to the court, which revealed Mandy's and Damien's involvement in a prostitution ring.

We were called back to family court more than one year after our first appearance when all the evaluations by the guardian ad litem and psychologist were done. Our lawyer informed us we needed to be prepared to go to trial. Our worst fear had materialized: Mandy was still contesting. We had hoped for an out of court settlement. We remained strong in our convictions and knew we had to continue seeking custody for the girls' sake. The hearing was at 10 a.m. Mandy wasn't there but the judge decided to start the proceedings without her. I was called to the stand first. I had previous experience in the courts as a child protection social worker, but this was my first time in a role of the plaintiff. I was so nervous I was shaking! The attorney did a good job through her questioning to establish our relationship, our concerns, and our desire to help our granddaughters.

Then Mrs. Bench, the guardian ad litem, who had previously taken a strong stand against us, followed with questions for me on some specifics of the report from the May incident when we took Mandy and the girls to our home after Mandy and Damien's altercation. Mandy had returned to their apartment during the night, leaving the girls behind at our place. I stated that the girls came out of the bedroom with only t-shirts on, and no underpants.

At that moment, an hour and a half late, Mandy walked into the courtroom. She looked tired, disheveled, and belligerent. She gave the judge some excuse for being late. The guardian interrupted me and asked for a recess.

Mandy, her attorney, and the guardian left the courtroom for a meeting while we were sent to the lobby. We could hear Mandy yelling from the closed room, and wondered what was happening.

Court reconvened about one half hour later. I noticed there were now two armed policemen in the courtroom. The judge called the court to order. She stated that the court social worker, our attorney, and the guardian had conferred on all the findings and had unanimously made a recommendation to the court. The Judge ruled that we be given permanent legal physical custody of the girls until they were 18 years of age. We had not even asked for this. We had asked for temporary full physical custody. The very guardian who had spoken strongly against us had recommended to the court that we be given custody! This was an unexpected turn of events.

Our lawyer Rita had been right in her request for the detailed records because the Judge and the attorneys had time ahead of the court date to study and evaluate the entire history. The detailed report brought about a more timely settlement for us, and we were grateful for Rita's expertise.

I believe that Mandy's behavior that day, along with the psychologist's report of Mandy's admission of prostitution helped to seal the court's decision. We were given immediate custody plus a police escort to our car.

Many restrictions and directives were written into the court order outlining the things Mandy needed to accomplish to regain custody of her daughters. She was ordered to get counseling, have supervised visitation, and have random drug tests. Whoever she lived with had to prove he was a law-abiding citizen for a period of six months, with no charges or arrests for anything! Mandy was also directed to complete a chemical dependency evaluation.

Mandy had brought Jewel with her to the courtroom. Jewel was immediately turned over to our care. Tyesha was at half-day kindergarten. We were directed to call the police and request an escort and meet the school bus. The court felt Damien was very dangerous.

We did call the police but the bus got to the bus stop first, before the police escort arrived. Thankfully, we had no trouble getting Tyesha from the school bus.

We learned after the hearing that Mandy and Damien had a reported police incident for domestic abuse earlier that week. The police report given to the judge before the court convened indicated that Mandy had chased Damien down the street with a baseball bat at 2 a.m.

On the way home the girls began giggling and wiggling in the back seat. It turned into a fight and they began spitting at each other. We stopped the car to settle them down. Terry turned to me laughing, "Now, tell me WHO won in court?" He was kidding, because we were very relieved to have our grandchildren in the safety of our home, but he also realized this was going to be a long journey for our family.

15

Getting On With Life

Now we had full custody of Mandy's two daughters after four years of Mandy and the girls enduring abusive relationships. We had become a statistic, without knowing it. We read that four million grandparents are raising their grandchildren. The Gerontologist states that more than 1 in 10 grandparents have been found to have cared for a grandchild for at least 6 months with most of them having engaged with a far longer commitment (Fuller-Thomson, E., Minkler, M., & Driver, D., 1996).

What has gone wrong? Why have so many families landed in this situation of family derailment? I see several pieces to the puzzle of this crisis. Some pieces are mental illness, addictions, immaturity, co-dependence, irresponsibility and rebellion. These are some of the reasons grandparents "step in" and "take over". There are some questions for each family to consider:

Is this the best plan for the grandchildren?

Do I have the stamina for daily life?

How will this affect my relationship with my own adult children?

How will this affect my marriage relationship?

Are both grandparents in agreement?

Has God called us to do this?

We were now in for the long haul of daily care and responsibility for both our granddaughters' development. We were elated to have Tyesha and Jewel, we felt honored that God trusted us with them. Our hearts rested knowing they were in a safe place, our home.

The granddaughters had been coming every other weekend for three years. Jenna was eighteen and Todd was thirteen when the girls moved in permanently. This decision affected Jenna and Todd profoundly. They supported us but surely paid an emotional price to have the family dynamics change.

Tyesha was six years old and Jewel was five when we were given full physical custody of them. The court ordered family counseling for the girls. We immediately began taking them to a Child Guidance Clinic for weekly sessions, regarding neglect and abuse, including sexual abuse. They did play therapy weekly. I always attended the sessions with them. Their counselor said that the girls were removed at a critical time in their development. He said they were at the end of the "formative" time, where a child learns the difference between right and wrong. He felt we had gotten them out in the nick of time to influence their lives with a sense of morality.

Our counselor watched the girls as they played with characters in the playhouse. They would play with the dolls and "act out" certain behaviors. He asked them what was going on (like a man and woman fist fighting). And then he would speak appropriate responses to the situation they described. He talked with the girls about appropriate sexual behaviors for men and women, like not having kids come in a room where people are naked. He talked about our bodies, and their privacy, and whom it was appropriate to show ourselves to. We counseled like this for one and a half years.

Observing the counseling sessions was an extreme emotional drain for me, but I was grateful there was this type of help for them. I wished with all my heart they had not been exposed to such things, in their time of innocence. They were so young to be exposed to such mature subjects, but all my wishing didn't make the fact go away. We had to deal with reality, and trust God to heal our grandchildren's memories.

The counselor had to report the abuse to Child Protection services. The girls had to be interviewed for evaluation of the abusive events. The process was to determine whether or not criminal charges should be brought against all the perpetrators. The evaluation concluded that the girls had been sexually molested, but in the opinion of the investigators, the girls' testimonies would not be strong enough to bring a conviction. They were considered poor witnesses because of their ages.

I believe physical and sexual abuse needs to be addressed in a cognitive way, as well as on an emotional and a spiritual level, with those who have been molested. My personal belief is that no permanent healing comes without healing the spirit of the victim! God is able to heal the memories, relieve the guilt and shame and bring measurable restoration to the abused victim through the healing power of the Holy Spirit. The victim needs to address the emotions felt at the time of abuse with a trusted counselor or clergy, to forgive the perpetrator, and invite God to heal. I believe the spiritual residue between the victim and the perpetrator needs to be addressed with God as the healer. I have personally counseled many ladies in this area, and have seen great freedom for those who renounce this connection made during the sexual contact.

To 'renounce' is to say formally, out loud, that I give up any residue or attachment that experience left with me. I speak out and break any soul ties with the person spiritually. A 'soul tie' is when our flesh, emotions, or minds are still connected to that person or experience. An example of renouncing is if a person has been raped, they may say, "I break any connection or soul ties made with me during that experience. I am under the protection of Jesus Christ and His shed blood, and I will no longer allow that person to hold me back or hurt me. I break any connection from Satan with that person, in Jesus' name."

Abuse within relationships comes in many ways. There is emotional abuse connected with all other forms of abuse. Many individuals believe that sexual abuse is the worst abuse; however, the most damaging of abuses is that of verbal abuse. The individual who is verbally abused incorporates the words as part of their own description of self and uses them repeatedly against themselves. The older, bigger person (whether parent or another child) speaking the names and accusations is accepted by a child as knowing what they are talking about. The child accepts the words as truth. Sexual abuse is perhaps the most confusing of abuses in that the child may see these events as the only times they receive individual attention and affection, so they may even become promiscuous and seductive in an attempt to get more of this hands on nurturing, even if it is confusing to them. The physical responses of sexual abuse may also be confusing when the physical touching gives pleasure and the child's innocence is destroyed. Sexual curiosity may be awakened before their bodies are ready for sexual relationships. This curiosity may lead them to abuse other children in their search of exploration and understanding. Physical abuse is the most recognizable, as there is bruising and broken bones as evidence for others to see.

> *"The body is not meant for sexual immorality, but for the Lord and the Lord for the body. By His power God raised the Lord from the dead and He will raise us also. Do you not know that your bodies are members of Christ Himself? Shall I then take the members of Christ and unite them with a prostitute? Never! Do you not know that he who unites himself with a prostitute is one with her in body? For it is said, the two shall become one flesh. But he who unites himself with the Lord is one with Him in Spirit. Flee from sexual immorality. All other sins, a man commits are outside his body, but he who sins sexually sins against his own body. Do you not know that your body is a temple of the Holy Spirit who is in you, who you have received from God?"* 1 Corinthians 6:13b-20a

Mandy did not once visit the girls in the first year they were living in our home. There were occasional phone calls. I arranged for Mandy to meet us at our local Perkins for Tyesha's 7th birthday. The girls were so excited to be seeing their mom.

When Mandy arrived she came walking in, talking on her cell phone. Both girls ran to her excitedly, grabbing her as she proceeded to talk on her phone. Most of the conversation at the restaurant was about her. Both girls were so angry when we got home. Lots of hugs, listening, and reassuring were needed to settle them down once we got home. In retrospect I see it was a totally codependent move on my part to arrange the visit. In an Al-Anon group I learned that one definition of control is "when we want something for someone more than they want it themselves, and we try to make it happen!" I wanted Mandy to become a caring parent. I was trying to protect the girls from rejection, and it backfired. I think speaking truth to the girls at that time would have been a better choice. Their Mom was fully consumed with herself!

16

A Word in Time

After the girls came permanently to our home, Mandy and Damien split. Mandy was homeless for a time, but found a new boyfriend named James who provided housing for her. Mandy appeared to be continuing her dangerous lifestyle. My heart was still aching. There was nothing I could do to change her, except pray. There were some days prayer did not seem like enough, yet I knew God wanted more for us, Mandy and the girls.

During the second year of our custody of the girls, we went to a family wedding. I was talking with a cousin who was upset because his nineteen-year-old son had gotten his ear pierced. The dad was embarrassed and upset by his son's lack of conformity.

I listened and thought to myself, "Baby you have nothing to worry about compared to what we deal with!"

I even laughingly said to him, "Hey, at least your kid's name isn't in the paper!" I don't know why I said that. I guess I was remembering when my brother's name was in the paper for breaking and entering a junkyard. I remembered the shame I felt at that time as a family member.

Two days later, my sister called to tell me there was a story in the paper that would be *of interest* to me. She said, "Your daughter was named in the article."

I opened my daily paper to read of a *prostitution ring* that had been busted in a neighboring suburb and there was Mandy's name. I was shocked and shamed to see Mandy's name. She was still doing the same thing, even two years after losing custody of her children.

I called Mandy, and asked, "What is the story in the newspaper about?"

"It was nothing! Just bug off, Mom. I am already getting enough grief from James!" her current boyfriend.

She didn't deny the charges, but added, "I needed some money for Christmas gifts." She insisted, "I really didn't *do* anything!"

This is another one of those times when I blew it as a parent. I was furious with her, and her lack of remorse. I suggested, "Why don't you change your last name, so you don't drag us through the mud with you!"

She had given us a foot massager for a Christmas gift. There was no way I would keep it, knowing where she had gotten the money. We donated it to a thrift shop.

About two weeks later I asked the Lord what I should read. I seemed to hear, "Read Matthew Chapter 1." I opened my Bible thinking, "What am I going to get from *this*? It's just Jesus' genealogy!" I read each word while asking, "Lord, what do you want me to get from this?"

I'm reading "Ram the father of Amminadab, Amminadab, the father of Nashon, Nashon the father of Salmon, Salmon the father of Boaz, Boaz whose mother was Rahab."

And then I knew: "Yes! There it was, Rahab. I remembered. Rahab the *harlot* was in Jesus' family line." I almost burst into tears. Wait a minute; one of Jesus' ancestors was a prostitute?

Once again, God knew my deepest thoughts, and wanted to minister His peace and love to me. If Jesus could have a prostitute in His family line, I guess I should accept one in my family line.

Oh God, thank you for showing me; thank you for correcting me; thank you that *You are* the God of restoration and *redemption*. My heart sang for days, knowing God knew all this about my thoughts about Mandy, but He loved her, and me enough to correct me, and not let my heart sit in judgment of her.

Studying God's word helps me because it is practical and useful for my everyday life. The miraculous part of this is the timing! God gives me the words so pertinent to the daily changing concerns of my heart. Who would have thought there were words of comfort in there for a mom grieving over her child's choice of "prostitution" as a way of making money?

Mandy has never told me but I assume this is where she got her "felony" record that plagues her until this day. God has allowed her to get jobs in spite of it. He is on her side, because He is a Father who has created us to have "fellowship" with Him.

Todd's huge heart of mercy was on overload, with all the uncertainty in our lives. Todd loved his sister a lot, and was concerned for her safety, but had conflicted feelings about her irresponsibility. He witnessed firsthand the hardship Mandy's decisions made on our entire family. His world was the most affected by the grandchildren living in our home, as their ages were closest to his age.

Nightmares were a regular part of the girls' lives the first two years they lived with us. They had frightening sexual dreams. Either we prayed at their bedside or sometimes their only comfort was to come to us and cuddle in our bed. Sometimes they wanted to sleep on the floor beside our bed. Our prayers were always fervent and pleading, "God help heal these little lambs. Protect them from the chaos."

I would be so angry at Mandy for having allowed sexual abuse in the girl's lives. Then I would ask God's forgiveness, and pray healing for Mandy and the girls. By age seven, the sexual dreams were really bothering Jewel. I praised God she was forthright and trusting enough to tell us about them.

She admitted playing a sexual game with Tyesha. Whenever they would "signal" each other from their beds they would have "sex play" together. They had been sexually aroused so early in their lives. These physical responses were awakened. Tyesha had been reportedly "humping" toys and other kids in the foster home at age 16 months.

This humping is a type of masturbation and not a natural behavior for a toddler. Such action would only be a result of manipulation, i.e., sexual abuse by someone older, or a child also previously abused. Sexual manipulation of children destroys their innocence and awakens awareness of their sexuality far before the naturally prescribed time for such an awakening.

The challenge was to teach them about their sexuality without shame. We wanted to teach them Godly values about sex. Jewel seemed to have the most understanding that the sex play was not appropriate behavior for her and Tyesha. She was the one who told me about their sex play.

I asked our Pastor to meet with Terry, the girls and me. We wanted the Pastor to hear their stories, so that he could pray with understanding for them. They told him how they would pull their nightgowns up, and signal each other to engage in their activities. Pastor spoke with them about sexual responses, and prayed with them for healing of memories, and to forgive those who abused them. I felt they needed deliverance from a perverse sexual spirit. This spirit preys on victims of sexual abuse. A woman in our church specialized in deliverance prayer. We met with her and the girls and prayed to bind sexual spirits named as "incubus and succubus" from them (Sanford, 2009, p. 44).

Both girls reported less inclination and the dreams stopped. They slept peacefully for a long time after that. Over time we saw them settle down. They got to a place where they slept through the night peacefully. Each girl was in their own bedroom at this time.

I taught them to be very careful of what they watched, and read, because the desires, impulses and spirits would come back with any pornographic viewing. I explained to them pornography and unhealthy sexual behavior would be an area of their lives they would always have to guard themselves against because of what had happened to them so early in their lives.

I explained that the sexual release was for marriage. We spoke with them about how God created us for a special relationship of two committed people, called marriage. How hard it was to have to talk about such adult things to children. As I stated earlier I believe sexual abuse needs to be addressed on a physical, emotional, and spiritual level for complete healing to occur. I also asked our other children not to have the girls babysit for them because their sexual exposure would place them in a place of dangerous temptation and put the other grandchildren at risk. I told the girls I felt I had a responsibility to tell our other kids. They accepted this. Our adult children who lived in our city were upset with us. Truth is not always convenient!

We enrolled the girls in our neighborhood school. Tyesha's counselor diagnosed her as ADHD in second grade. Terry and I went to a workshop for parenting kids with ADHD. While we were in class, the girls were in a group that was run by a therapist. Tyesha told the group of second graders about her dad being in prison, her mom almost being killed by him and a few other alarming stories. The school therapist was alarmed and pulled us aside after the class and asked if all this was true. I said most of it was, unfortunately, and the girls had had much counseling. The therapist felt the girls needed more help, and the school district offered to pay, so we gladly accepted the help.

We had helpful counsel from a child psychologist who came to our home weekly. Tyesha struggled with erupting emotions over any stress in her life. During one of the visits, the psychologist drew a thermometer on a large piece of paper, and numbered it from one to ten, ten being at the top. She explained to Tyesha most events should elicit a two or a three in emotions. Rarely would emotions escalate to a ten in intensity. Then she spoke with Tyesha about her dramatic responses to most situations. She taught Tyesha to think about the situation, and decide if it was a one, a three, or a ten on the emotional thermometer.

Tyesha seemed to grasp this concept quite well, because when something would agitate her I'd ask her "Is it a 3 or a 7?"

She'd grin and say, "I guess it's a 3," as she settled down.

This word picture concept helped us communicate with Tyesha. It was a good visual to use with Tyesha when she would come in the house, very agitated about a situation. The visual thought of numbering the severity of the event actually brought Tyesha and I to laughter sometimes. It was a good tool to help her deescalate her emotions. Even in her early twenty's she is still trying to master her emotions appropriately by taking anger management classes.

Three years after the girls came to our home, Mandy entered counseling. She progressed to a point of even arranging for Tyesha's 8th birthday party at a party center near us. Mandy had missed the other birthdays. By this time it seemed to us she had gotten to a new place of caring about her girls. She was calling to talk to the girls on the phone regularly. She made all the party arrangements, got the cake and even paid for everything. She had gifts that were appropriate, and was actually engaging in the girls' lives. We were finally seeing progress, and thanked God for it.

17

Nevertheless

Terry started doing personal day retreats for himself when he was in the middle of a job change, and wanted to seek the Lord's direction. After these retreats, he came home so peaceful and confident that I decided this would be a good thing for me to do too. I made a practice of going to a retreat for myself twice a year and it was time for me to go again. We were in the middle of raising the two grandchildren, Todd walking through depression, and Jason's divorce; so, one spring day I went to Mount Mary Retreat Center for a day of prayer.

I was weary, and felt depleted of energy and desire. I wanted to parent with joy and enthusiasm. I went there looking for strength and renewed hope and vision to continue parenting the two grandchildren, along with our two children still at home.

My practice was to read the Bible until something jumped off the page for me, or really intrigued me. I was reading 1 Kings15:1-9. It's the story of King David's descendants, namely David's grandson Abijah, and how he was not following God the way they had been taught.

> "He [Abijah] committed all the sins his father had done before him; his heart was not fully devoted to the Lord his God, as the heart of David his forefather had been. *Nevertheless*, for David's sake the Lord his God gave him a lamp in Jerusalem by raising a son to succeed him and by making Jerusalem strong." 1 Kings 15:3-4

When I came to the word "*nevertheless*", my heart started to beat faster, and I knew the Holy Spirit had something to say to me. It was so encouraging. In this story God was remaining faithful to David regardless of what his descendant had done. God was honoring His word to stay with David's family line, because David had remained faithful to God. One word, one Holy Spirit inspired word; the word "*nevertheless*" was able to lift me to a new place, a better place, a place of joy and hope, and purpose. I was able to go home strengthened in my inner person to continue with what I believed God had called us to do.

> "The words I have spoken to you are spirit and they are life." John 6:63b

My retreat time in the Bible certainly had done its work in my life at that moment, giving me the life and energy to continue parenting our family and the grandchildren. Even though King David's family wasn't faithful, God was and *is* faithful. God didn't just look at the grandson, but looked to the faithful life of the elder in the family. This passage said to me that no matter what was going on in my family's life today, "nevertheless," God was still on the throne, and His promise to help my family was good. I was refreshed, energized, renewed, and ready to go home and serve my family again.

Here is an excerpt from my journal, "Feelings, Lord; how utterly fickle they are! Mine change constantly! From tired, weary, sad, hopeless this morning, to victorious, strong, and encouraged this afternoon. What did it? Focusing on God's Word! This morning I focused on the problems, the relationships, and saw no change. This afternoon I read your Word and saw and felt the power of You acting in someone's life. I know I can always be at your banqueting table, like Mephiboseth was. (Jonathan's only surviving child: 2 Sam.4:4-9). Please help me remember this Jesus."

Early in my Christian walk a mentor reminded me how fickle feelings can be, and not to think they are necessarily truth. They can change so quickly. She encouraged me to use the Word of God as my compass, *not* my feelings. This has been a very useful guideline for me, and it has saved me from some potentially harmful "reactions." Lord knows I've done enough of that along the way. We made plenty of mistakes based on angry outbursts and emotional ranting that weren't mature and Godly responses.

My goal is to get to the place where I live and lead from principles, not from reactions. Hosea was the perfect model of this in the Old Testament. God called him to live with an unfaithful wife, to keep responding to her in love, regardless of her behavior. This is an example of God's unconditional love and mercy for Israel, His chosen people, and for us. God tells us to forgive each other seventy times seven times. I have found I must always forgive. My challenge is to decide whether to reengage again, or to remove myself from the situation. God used a delicate balance of both unconditional love and tough love in His dealings with Israel, his chosen people.

18

Chad Parenting

A one-day retreat rejuvenated me but life continued for our family.

After Chad went away to the state college we seldom heard from him. I would call occasionally, but he didn't want much to do with us. We had confronted his marijuana use and Chad deeply resented us for it. He stayed away from home for almost two years.

We grew concerned as well over Chad's four year relationship with a young woman, Leah. We liked her and her family a lot. She seemed to be a pleasant, hardworking, attractive young lady, but I suspected she and my son were sleeping together the weekends she visited him at college. One afternoon during the summer after Leah graduated from high school, I invited her over for a "heart to heart talk." I asked her to stop this behavior because of the possibility of an unplanned pregnancy. Leah assured me that she and Chad had discussed this and he had promised to marry her if she ever got pregnant.

Later that fall Chad called saying, "I have good news and bad news. May I come home to talk to you?"

We were anxious about what was up with our son as we waited for his arrival at our home.

Chad asked, "Which do you want first? The good news or the bad news?"

"Good news, of course," we responded.

Chad announced, "The good news is that Leah is pregnant."

I said "Oh."

"The bad news is we broke up last week."

I wasn't too concerned, "This is just a lover's quarrel."

Chad strongly declared, "We are not getting back together, no matter what."

That was the end of the discussion. Chad was very emphatic.

I waited patiently thinking surely any day Chad would come home with Leah on his arm. That day never came. Months went by with no change in his posture on the breakup.

We later found out the truth. Chad already had another girlfriend.

Our expectations for our kids were continuing to crumble before our eyes. Our eldest was in the middle of divorce and we had custody of our second child's two daughters - our granddaughters. Our third son was refusing to marry the mother of his child. Our life was not working out as we wanted it to. Our ideal family was not ideal nor was it even happy at this time. There were broken dreams flooded with many tears; but we were still a family of intertwined lives. The troubled waters did not quench our love for our children.

Chad's child, our third beautiful grandchild entered the world. She was darling, olive skinned like daddy and petite featured like mom. Chad was extremely proud of his baby. It was fulfilling to see him be excited about someone. He had been in the delivery room with Leah and shared with us his awe of the experience of witnessing his child's birth. I was glad he was there physically for Leah, at least during the delivery. Chad seemed genuinely happy with his new daughter, even though he was now living with a new girlfriend Sue.

Chad said he'd be having his baby Tara stay with him and Sue in his apartment every other weekend. I was really nervous about this because Chad had always been a very sound sleeper when he lived at home. You could hardly rouse him in the morning. What if the baby cried and he didn't hear her, just like Mandy? I expressed this concern to both Chad and Leah, but neither felt it would be an issue. It was a time to trust the Lord's hand over another grandchild. Chad worked it all out with Leah and he began seeing Tara regularly, taking full responsibility for the baby's care on his weekends. I was amazed thinking most dads wouldn't want full care of a newborn for entire weekends. Chad brought Tara to our home for his mid-week visitations. We loved this time with him and our grandchild. I admired Chad's gentle attentiveness with his child. The visitation on Wednesdays continued for two years until he married Sue, his new girlfriend.

Sue wanted to assume the role of mother to Tara. Chad was in a "catch 22" position of his own making torn between the baby and two women. Sue, now his wife, wanted to mother Tara, but Leah, the birth mom, reacted angrily. Chad, quiet and reserved, caught the wrath from both sides. Sue felt she had a mother's rights because she had cared for Tara on the visitation weekends and wanted to be accepted by Leah, the baby's mom. Sue wanted the two moms, Chad, and the baby to be one happy family. I explained to Chad's new wife Sue that Tara already had a mom and didn't need another one.

God knows the wrath of a jealous woman. I suggested to Sue that she was the "other woman" in this story, and Leah probably saw her as the direct cause of her pain and rejection by Chad. Sue never understood. We watched her suffer much anxiety in trying to build a friendly relationship with Leah, Tara's biological mom.

> "Anger is cruel and fury is overwhelming but who can stand before jealousy?" Proverbs 27:4

Our life felt like a soap opera. How could a Godly Christian family have so many problems? Terry and I felt like failures as parental role models for our children. We prayed constantly, wanting to protect them from pain, and yet we watched each one in so much turmoil.

> "Even though the fig trees are all destroyed and there is neither blossom left nor fruit, and though the olive crops all fail, and the fields are barren, even if the flocks die in the field, and the cattle barns are empty, yet will I rejoice in the Lord. I will be glad in the God of my salvation." Habbakuk 3:17-18

Our family certainly seemed to fit this description of barrenness and I did not feel like rejoicing. I felt Satan's constant harassment that I was a failure as a parent, and had to set my mind on things above at many times, to stay focused on God's promises for our family instead of the natural circumstances. I knew the negative thoughts about myself were *not* the truth, because I did not make the choices, our adult children had. We continued to follow Christ to the best of our ability. Certainly we could always improve in our communication and love. We had not failed completely.

> "Though He slay me yet will I serve Him." Job 13:15a

These verses seemed to describe my life, barren of any fruit and yet I was called on to praise God, so I did. I thanked Him for health, for life, for each day He gives us. I felt overwhelmed and discouraged many times because of our children's choices. We felt that our parenting throughout their lives had been fruitless. We had great personal pain while watching what was happening in their lives. I purposed to serve God for there was nowhere else for me to find comfort. He had been faithful to me in the past, and I had to trust Him with each of these situations.

Chad and Sue married after living together for two years. They floundered from the beginning. Chad actually called the wedding off one month before the date. When we heard the wedding was back on as scheduled earlier, I called Chad and said, "Son don't worry about what anyone thinks, if you don't want to marry Sue, you need to follow your heart on this!"

Chad assured me he was ready to commit and now wanted to go forward with the wedding. The ceremony was lovely. Chad was handsome in his tux and the bride was radiant. It was a beautiful reception. Chad had many friends there celebrating. Even though there was a disc jockey, our son Chad disengaged from the celebration, and ran the sound system while everyone else danced. Sue danced not with her groom but with others. It was hard to watch the couple and not worry about their future.

We found out later Chad had made no wedding night or honeymoon arrangements. They had to scurry to find a hotel. I felt ashamed that my son was disrespectful to his bride and didn't provide for her. I was sad for both of them. We had not raised him to treat a woman this way.

About four months into the marriage Sue came to see us, and sobbed her heart out. She was confused by Chad's behavior. She said he was so hard to live with. He had quit his job and would leave in the middle of the night and was gone for hours. Chad's story was that he couldn't sleep and so he went to visit his friends and play video games.

I suspected this behavior was drug related. I asked Sue to go with me to a class called SAFE at our local hospital. SAFE is an acronym for Substance Abuse Family Education. We sat in a room full of people, most of whom had been court ordered to be there. The speaker described what drug use and abuse looks like played out in daily life: namely money unaccounted for, unaccountable behaviors, unusual hours, disturbed sleep, and job struggles.

On the way home I asked Sue if this was the issue they were facing. She replied, "No. Marijuana isn't habit forming and he only uses a little." We were offering to help Sue do an intervention with our son, but she did not feel it was necessary.

Chad played the victim role in his relationships with the two women. We were frustrated, watching Chad working only part time. Sue and Chad had both assured us that when working in the food service industry it was common practice to have 25 hour weeks. Since Sue and Chad were satisfied, we had no more to say.

Later we learned from our other adult children that Sue blamed us totally for their marriage problems, saying we had never taught Chad how to handle money. This was not true. Our motto has always been "pay as you go" with no credit card debt. Both of us worked our way through college, and took any job we could get, to earn money for school. After attending a Mirror Images retreat* I confronted Sue about her allegations. We had a healing time, forgiving each other, after revisiting the pain we had both experienced during that time.

Chad did come to one counseling session with me when I was diagnosed with cancer. I also felt a great measure of reconciliation with Chad about our woundedness through the Mirror Image program, which I made four years later. We exchanged letters that allowed us to address some of our hurts with each other. At least they were on the table, which gave us opportunity for healing.

* *Mirror Images is a group program of personal confrontation with self. The program has five stages of exploration and discovery.*

123

Each individual scrutinizes their own life, receiving input and evaluation for truth from the other group members. Most individuals survive their childhood conflicts by normalizing, but the others in the group are able to identify abuse and pain more easily than the one who has endured the events. The Mirror Image process includes:

1. *Generational Exploration (Family Genealogy)*

2. *Historical Perspective*

3. *Evaluation of Relationships*

4. *Personal Responsibility and Restoration*

5. *Looking Ahead*

Further information can be found at www.mirrorimagesretreats.org

19

Reunion in Prison

After the first three years Tyesha and Jewel lived with us, I thought it was time for them to learn more about their birth father. I was of the opinion that truth always prevails.

> "You shall know the truth and the truth shall set you free!" John 8:32

Mandy was not visiting the girls at this time. We had helped Jason, Mandy and Jenna find their birth parents. Having heard that many adopted children, ours included, had questions about what their birth parents were like, I wanted Tyesha and Jewel to "know" their father. We wanted them to have some knowledge of their roots. We had always prayed for the girls' dad, who everyone affectionately called "Peanut." I learned he was at a correctional facility in a nearby suburb.

I went through the necessary paper work to be allowed to visit him. I went alone for the first visit, to discern whether it would be a good idea for them to visit. My first time inside a prison facility, I found I had to pass through three locked doors before getting to the visitors room. By then, I was feeling choked with the loss of my freedom and overwhelmed at the thought of how many times Peanut had been through these doors! I wondered how he could endure this.

The visiting room was stark, long and narrow with grey metal folding chairs facing each other in two rows about two feet apart. Guards sat in an elevated station in every corner of the room so they could observe what was going on, watching like hawks all those in the visitation area.

Peanut walked into the room. His changed appearance took my breath away. He was huge, muscular, bushy haired, and had the physique of a weight lifter. The last time I saw him, he had been a tall, skinny, lanky looking teen. Now he looked like Goliath to me. He looked at me skeptically at first, but then a big grin came over his face. He sauntered over and sat down across the aisle from me.

It had been about seven years since I'd last seen him. The guards shouted at us as we shook hands. "You are not to touch each other!"

We sat there face to face. I was thinking to myself, "This is the man who tried to murder my daughter! What *am* I doing here?" I knew both Mandy and Peanut had been using drugs at the time, so there was no animosity in my heart. Both had been wrong. Mandy had told us many times that he had not intended to kill her. Otherwise I probably could not have faced him.

Peanut started out by saying that he still loved Mandy, but they just couldn't get along! He said he really loved his "little shorties," as he affectionately called the girls. He asked about them, and whether we had given them the letter he had written them. We had. That letter was very poetic and filled with flowery loving thoughts. I could hardly believe the man I was looking at wrote it! It was surprising to read the tender expressions he wrote to the girls; this man had been in and out of jail and prison since he was fourteen years old. By looking at him, one would think he had no tender emotions in him at all! This was far from what I was about to discover about him.

We talked freely. I asked him to tell me about himself. He said he lost every job he had ever gotten in prison because he always got angry and exploded. As a result he had no money, and asked if we would buy him some personal hygiene products. We did this twice, and then declined, letting him deal with the consequences of his behaviors.

Peanut said he had a short fuse.

I told him of Tyesha's ADHD, describing some of her behaviors. He laughed again, saying she sounded just like him. I explained ADHD was a brain disorder that could be improved with medicine and education. I encouraged him to learn about ADHD, suggesting he talk to the prison doctor. If he could be tested maybe he would find some relief for the "anger" issues. We talked about the possibility of the right medicine helping him live more peacefully. I said it could also be the key to keeping him away from using street drugs. I left the prison with a new understanding about some of the issues we had experienced with the girls.

I told him about Bible classes offered through Prison Fellowship. This organization also offers educational classes on anger management, how to re-enter society, and how to deal with family issues. He seemed interested, so I sent his name to Prison Fellowship but I have no idea if he ever followed up on it.

Peanut began to tell me the "saga" of his life. He started by saying his dad taught him to be a pimp. His dad had been his mom's pimp, "That was all I ever knew how to do!" Peanut said he has a brother two years older, and they both have been in and out of prison most of their adult lives. He laughingly said, "We were even in at the same place together once!" He found that pretty funny. My heart ached for him, for myself, and for his children, my grandchildren!

Peanut said he was born in a small town in the south. His mom used drugs and didn't take care of him. He told me about the times he and his brother roamed the streets of town at the ages of three and four, looking for food and someone to care for them. Finally their grandmother took them in. Then, by age eleven, Grandma couldn't handle them anymore so she sent them to his dad in Colorado.

Peanut told me he first went to detention at age fourteen, when he "sliced a girl's arm up real bad, at a Burger King". I had heard from one of our relatives who worked in corrections that he was in a sex offenders program so I asked him about this. He insisted he was "only in for violence", not anything sexual.

Peanut said he was eager to "get out and get a job". He showed me a photo of two more of his children who live in Chicago. The photo was taken in a dark dingy corner of a house. The kids looked dirty, and like they were definitely living at a poverty level. Their ages looked close to Tyesha and Jewel's, around 3 to 4 years old. Peanut said he has at least two other children, so, counting our girls, he has six children that we're aware of!

Peanut liked art and poetry. He showed me a lovely long stem rose he had made for the girls. The rose was made from toilet paper, which was quite amazing and looked very real. He asked if I would bring the girls to see him, so I agreed to talk to them about it!

Peanut told of a time when he brought Mandy and eight month old Tyesha to meet his mom. I remembered Mandy telling me they had done this. It was one of those many times I had prayed for God's protection over them. Peanut said they went out partying and left Tyesha with his mom, Grandma Williams. Grandma was furious that his girlfriend was white. When they came home they found cigarette burns on Tyesha's upper leg and back. Peanut said he was so angry with his mom that they left immediately, never to see her alive again.

I remembered Mandy calling me to say Peanut's mom had died, at the age of 37, stabbed to death by her boyfriend. She had refused to give him her paycheck for drug money. Peanut was 23 years old when his mother was murdered.

When I heard this story my heart went out to Peanut. I told him God loved him, and had a better plan for his life. I explained God never wanted any of that to happen to him. We cried together. He said he would go to the Bible studies offered at the prison. Several years before this he had been incarcerated at the County Jail, and I had sent a friend who is a chaplain to talk to him. My friend reported that Peanut was very resistive at first, but eventually let him pray with him.

I recall the guard yelling at us, and correcting us for "laughing" too loud at one point. When that happened Peanut tightened every muscle in his face and started to get up, to "punch the guard out!" I told him to sit down, and let it go. I explained that he needed to learn to control himself and the impulsive behaviors. My visit helped me not be so judgmental of Peanut's choices, and once again, I was able to prayerfully place him in God's hand.

About one month later, I brought the girls to see their dad. He was very polite and appropriate with them. He smiled a lot commenting on how grown up they were. He had made an artificial rose for each of them out of toilet tissues. The girls were reticent and shy. I was pleased with their response because I had seen Tyesha be inappropriately friendly other times with strangers. They answered his questions but said little else. He thanked me for bringing them. I truly have no idea if that helped or hindered them. The visit really helped me accept and process some of the behaviors I saw in the children, knowing their genetic roots.

God loves Peanut and his entire extended family, and we believe God wants to heal this family and restore them. We have great hope for two reasons. First, God spoke to me at a women's conference of over 2000. The speaker began her evening message by saying she had a word of knowledge for someone who was praying for a loved one in prison. She said, "The Lord says you are not to worry, God is moving in their heart." It was as if the words were carried on an arrow from her mouth to my heart. There was about a thirty second delay, and all of a sudden my heart started pounding, and I realized she was prophesying about Peanut. I leaned over to Krista and Katie, my foster daughters, and said, "That is me she is talking about and I think it's for Peanut!" They had the same witness in their hearts at the same time. Krista said, "God just told me it is for Peanut!" I don't know how or when but I am assured Peanut will serve God, because of that word and the prayers that go up for him. Secondly, Peanut's father has become a believer and is also praying for his son.

20

Grandparents Parenting

By Todd's junior year the depression had lifted and he was helpful around the house. He helped a lot with our two granddaughters now living with us. That summer he attended a ten-week discipleship training program at family Bible camp together with Krista's daughter. He also had a part-time job.

I needed help with my conflicted feelings towards my daughter, Mandy. We had the girls for over two years but Mandy hardly ever called to see how they were. When she did call she acted like everything was perfectly normal. She offered no financial support. She seemed to have no interest at all in their daily life. We did not know if she was working. I was trying to stay above bitterness and resentment.

The Lord kept reminding me of two things: First we chose to take care of the girls in an attempt to give them some stability. Our choice to parent our grandchildren was a deliberate decision. Secondly, I am a sinner too.

I read about a grandparent support group. I was desperate for some help. The next meeting was scheduled the night of a blizzard, but I determined to get there even if I had to crawl.

At first I loved the support group because it was a safe place to talk about many issues that I did not think my friends, neighbors, and the "church" people could understand. There were eight other grandparents at this meeting, along with a facilitator from Family Services.

I heard many tragic stories of frustration and disappointments from the grandparents as they shared all their efforts to reach their adult children. We were all frustrated in our attempts to make our child become an adult, and take responsibility for themselves and their children. Drugs were the most obvious culprits for robbing families of their sanity. (Later on, after taking a class on mental health issues, I realized that some of the adult children simply did not have the skill or ability to parent, because of mental health issues.) The grandparents, including myself, were hoping they could change their adult children. We were in denial of our lack of power or ability to change our adult children.

After four or five meetings I was no longer motivated to go. The meetings were open with no agenda and usually became a parade of all the troubles and accusations against the irresponsible adult child. There was a tone of "I am the savior, I'm the martyr, and they'll never change!" This did not line up with my Christian belief "with Christ all things are possible" but seemed to only increase the resentment I was already feeling!

I did learn how to get financial aid from the county, and initiate legal action against our granddaughters' father for support. He was out of jail at that time.

The group offered "play days" for the grandparents and kids together. These were very helpful as it was challenging to find fun things to do for both grandchildren and grandparents. This group also helped both the kids and us realize we weren't the only ones in this situation. There was daycare provided for the monthly meeting, so I would sometimes bring the girls so they could be with other children in similar circumstances. These groups are somewhat helpful because they provide a safe place where people are able to express their frustrations. I would have preferred some of the time given to some helpful educational presentations dealing with the inter-generational conflicts rather than just the unstructured sharing sessions.

During these years I spent a lot of time reading the Psalms in the Bible. There were many words of comfort and promises of help. I pleaded in my prayers for help to know how to meet my own needs.

Psalm 34:

"My soul will boast in the Lord; let the afflicted hear and be glad." v 2

"I sought the Lord and He answered me; He delivered me from all my fears." v 4

"The Lord is close to the brokenhearted and saves those who are crushed in spirit." v 18

I have Tyesha's name on one journal entry marked with this scripture, verse 18. She must have been struggling a lot at that time!

We arranged for our foster daughter Krista and her husband to take the girls for respite care. This gave Terry and I, and the other kids some down time every other weekend. There was also another dear Christian couple who did foster parenting who occasionally took the girls on weekends. We realized we needed some alone time with our son Todd and daughter Jenna.

Finally in our 4th year we switched roles, the girls lived with our foster daughter Krista and her family while we did respite care for them. We did this for 9 months, trying to sustain the commitment we had made to provide a safe place for the girls.

Todd recalls those years as being very difficult for him. He is mercy motivated and struggled seeing the girls in such pain. He also loved his sister Mandy very much, and wanted to see her life change for the better. Todd was caught between his loyalty toward his sister and his care for the children.

I believe grandparents act valiantly when they intervene and try to hold their families together. I have learned the Afro-American communities have done this through the generations. I certainly felt like I was laying down my own life for the girls. This took a lot of selfless love and grace. I don't think a family should consider it unless they feel directed by the Lord. There are so many hurdles and conflicting relationships between husband and wife, adult child, grandchildren and any children still in the home. The two hardest parts of the situation are first the grief and loss of our relationship with our own adult child; and, secondly, the pain we saw our grandchildren experience.

I believe we were able to do a much better job of parenting the grandchildren because of the things we learned from raising the other five children. We had more patience and understanding of the value of nurturing touch and words. The most wearing piece was dealing with the conflicting feelings of anger and hope toward our own child. We watched Mandy continually reject her daughters, our granddaughters. We wanted to protect the children, but learned that was not possible. We could only attempt to bring some comfort in their relationship with their mom that was filled with turmoil and uncertainty.

I don't regret one day of having my grandchildren live with me. I regret more that they didn't stay with us until they were older. I felt myself become emotionally depleted and understood this as God telling me it was time to "let go" of them; I was not their savior. We had custody of the girls for 5 years.

> "My grace is sufficient for you, for my power is made perfect in weakness." 2 Corinthians 12:9

My experience is that when God calls me He equips me to do the assignment with a measure of joy and peace. I had neither at that point in time.

21

Big Changes

We were still parenting Tyesha and Jewel. Jenna was training with a mission group. Todd was a junior in high school. Todd really disliked our church youth group, so during his junior year Todd and I agreed to do a Bible study at home, just the two of us. This worked well, for a time. The option of having a choice seemed to be really important to Todd. In one of our adoptive parenting classes at Family Service the social worker warned that control was a major issue for adopted children! She said they often feel they had no control over their lives as to why and where they are placed so they develop a high sensitivity to "being in control" of something.

Todd chose to enter the post-secondary program at his high school, going to college during his senior year of high school, earning college credits simultaneously, while getting his high school diploma. Todd loved being away from the high school scene and thrived at the junior college.

Todd said he was physically cold from the time we brought him home. He always said he was going to college where the weather was warmer. We had done a thyroid test at one point, to see if his metabolism was irregular. It was. Todd's answer to this issue was to move someplace warm to finish college and he chose Hawaii. Terry and I were aghast at having him that far away. We tried to discourage this move, challenging him that we'd be too far away to help in emergencies.

Todd did all the investigating, found an apartment, transferred his credits, saved his airfare, and away he went. In his second year there Terry and I went to visit him. We missed Todd and wanted to see his new home. We had never been to Hawaii. The first evening we walked down the street, thoroughly enjoying the balmy evening, the sound of the ocean, and the beauty of the island. Terry said, "I'm thinking my son is a lot smarter than me. If he's going to go to college, why not go someplace beautiful?" It was true. Todd graduated with a business degree. He took one semester off to be home with me when I went through chemotherapy for cancer. I was grateful, because he is very mercy motivated, and I needed all the TLC I could find during that crisis.

Todd lived in Hawaii for nine years. Living in the multi-cultural Asian population of Hawaii, he felt a great sense of belonging and more of a connection with the people around him. For the first time, when he looked around him he was in the majority not the minority. After graduating with a business major he took part-time jobs, which allowed flexibility and time for surfing rather than applying for a business position.

Back home the drama in Mandy's life continued. Every day with Mandy was a surprise. I was never sure what her next announcement would be. One day she called to say, "James and I are getting married on Wednesday."

I asked, "James who?"

"You know." He was the current boyfriend Mandy lived with for several years while we had the girls. I was glad Mandy and James wanted to make a commitment to each other. This call was on a Monday. They planned to go to the courthouse and marry before a judge on Wednesday.

I responded, "This is a special occasion, and Terry and I want to be there, if you want us." I offered our home as a place for the wedding. I said her brothers and sisters would like to see her wed also. She and James agreed so we started planning how to decorate our porch for the event. Mandy and I went shopping for a dress. This was rare for two reasons. We hardly ever shopped together, and Mandy rarely wore a dress. We had a lot of fun trying on dresses. This is one of my happier memories with Mandy. She is very flamboyant, and the styles she liked were unique. She chose a lovely blue gown with a long white coat. It felt so good to bless her and see her happy about herself and life.

One of my friends, Kathy, a talented decorator, offered to help make our porch look like a wedding chapel. Kathy transformed the space with lights, flowers, rented white chairs and tulle. All of us were pleased with the results. I think James and Mandy felt very special that day. A funny and remarkable "God thing" happened when the judge walked into our home. The Judge was a lady. She and James looked at each other, and smiled. James had just appeared before her several days beforehand! James told us he was "cleaning up" his act, and had turned himself in on some tickets, and gone to court. I could only hope it was true. And lo and behold, God sends the *very* Judge he had stood before, to our home, to confirm his clean record!

The ceremony was simple, vows spoken, Terry gave a blessing, and I read Psalm 139. This psalm talks about God knowing us in our mother's womb, how we are fearfully and wonderfully made, and how each day of our lives is planned before Him. James cried during the vows. This revealed to me James had a tender heart and had given thought to what he was doing!

We had asked James to invite his parents to the celebration but they declined; however, one of his sisters did come to our home. Our entire family, foster daughters, husbands and all went to a restaurant together after the ceremony. James' mom and step dad joined us there. It felt surreal to look over at the tables of the two families, thinking we had just joined our families. This was the first time we had talked to James' parents. They seemed very friendly, and gracious. We haven't seen them since. Later we learned that James did not want his mom at the ceremony because she has a drinking problem, and is unpredictable. He had no guarantee she wouldn't show up drunk, so he chose not to take the risk. He wanted his special day untainted. It was a good boundary for him.

After dinner, we went back to our house to open the wedding gifts and have wedding cake. James' family declined to join us. It was a beautiful day and a special time for us and Mandy.

22

Jenna Has a Baby

Our second daughter, Jenna, had been committed to missions early in her life and had spent three summers in foreign countries. After high school graduation she spent the next year working and training with a mission organization. Because of her commitment to God's work, we were stunned when Jenna became pregnant outside of marriage. She had only known the young man for three months. Her boyfriend Nate already had another child, and had told her he would only marry her if she placed this child for adoption.

Early in her pregnancy, Jenna and I had some really rough times. Jenna was extremely distraught because she was so disappointed in herself. She had never thought she would be in a position of being pregnant and not yet married. She was determined the father of her child be involved in her life despite the distance he was now setting between them. Jenna moved out of our home several months before the pregnancy occurred. Our relationship with her was volatile and we needed a break from the chaos of her angry outbursts. She was living with her best friend's family. They loved her and readily embraced her. We felt badly about asking her to move, but we needed space to heal our hearts to continue the relationship. We were unwilling to take the abusive anger from her.

During one discussion with Jenna during her pregnancy she lashed out at me saying, "You are just angry with me for getting pregnant. You are jealous because you were never able to conceive yourself."

These angry words hit me so hard my entire body shook with emotion. I was overwhelmed by the cruelty of her words. Without Jesus' love and forgiveness I would have crumbled. I did forgive her. We considered hospitalizing Jenna at one point in the pregnancy because she spoke of suicide. Our counselor called several hospitals to find an emergency bed, but none were available.

Jenna was so unstable she was sleeping in her car by the baby's father's home, waiting for him to come out in the morning. We begged her to stop dating Nate because he was unresponsive to her, and disrespectful of our rules. Her only reply was that she liked him because he was so handsome. We were concerned because he already had a child from another uncommitted relationship. He showed little respect for that child, our daughter or us.

Jenna began considering adoption. We kept praying for God's will in this situation. My heart was breaking for Jenna. I didn't want her to have to walk away from her child or to go through a loss of a grandchild myself. Yet I trusted God would provide the best solution for everyone. I knew He would guide Jenna, heal us all, and find a loving Christian home for the baby. We had been the adoptive parents and now we could be part of a birth family. This was not what I had pictured for my life.

Two months after Jenna's announcement of the pregnancy, I was as close to an emotional breakdown as I had ever been. Again, our lives were so broken, a chaotic mess. Terry was in the process of selling the business he managed. Our oldest was getting divorced, we were raising our daughter's children, our third son Chad had refused to marry the mother of his child, and now this.

I felt defeated as a Christian parent, trying to model Godly values to this family. I was emotionally worn out. A friend invited me to a weekend retreat at her church, so I could rest and regroup. At the retreat I heard several stirring testimonies of how God helped people through crisis. I was unmoved and tired. By the noon meal on Sunday I still hadn't heard any one thing that brought relief to my spirit.

At the noon meal on Sunday we were instructed to walk into the dining hall and take a seat at any table we chose. I knew no other women in the room, so I walked in and grabbed the first vacant seat available and sat down. Then we were instructed to pay close attention to our handmade placemat. My placemat was quite ordinary compared with some of the artistic creations I noted around me. But the words were just for me, this day, in this room, with the brokenness in my heart.

> "Be strong and courageous. Do not be terrified because of them, for the Lord your God goes before you. He will never leave you or forsake you." Deuteronomy 31:6

I received this as a rhema word from God. (A rhema word means a word spoken from the Bible specifically to a person for this moment in time.) At that moment God shouted into my heart His words of comfort.

My heart started to pound, tears came streaming down my cheeks; my "Daddy" had just spoken to my spirit, and my heart was overwhelmed with love, comfort, and gratitude. Once again, I was filled with hope for the future.

The picture drawn on the placemat was a mountain, very simply colored in brown and green. Other placemats were gorgeous artistic creations but mine was perfectly handpicked for me this day. The mountain was such a perfect picture of what I felt lay ahead for us as a family in our situation. My response to this was an immediate supernatural strength and calm, knowing God was with us in this crisis.

The verse was like a warm spring rain in the dry parched land of my soul. My heart absorbed it. This verse began to heal and hold my bruised and fearful heart. I wanted to shout, "Hey everybody, look how much God loves me. He's with me all the way."

From that point on I knew that whatever happened with Jenna and the baby, she would be okay, I would be okay, and the baby would be okay. God knew and He would give us His grace.

Anna was born at 4:30 a.m. on a summer day, after only two hours of labor. Jenna had refused to go to birthing classes, but God provided our foster daughter Krista as labor coach as she had been for Mandy, again helping me significantly in a time of need. Krista was so gentle and firm with Jenna. Jenna broke many blood vessels all over her face during the hard pushing of the labor. She was a hero in my eyes. I see Jenna and every birth mother as a hero. Delivery is hard work!

A special moment for me occurred during the delivery. Jenna was in the middle of a very hard contraction. She turned to me and said, "Mom I love you so much!"

I was surprised she even knew I was in the room, with all her labor pain! My heart was totally bonded to hers at that point. Here was my little girl, delivering a child herself. I could only imagine Jenna's turmoil of knowing the baby she was delivering was possibly going to be given to someone else. I was preoccupied about her adoption decision. Yet her love for me came through loud and clear in this moment. I had many mixed emotions going through this experience, watching Jenna give birth to her child. I felt honored to be present with Jenna at this sacred time of birth, and yet very sad thinking she would have to leave the baby behind in the hospital. Nate was present at the delivery but took a very passive role; at least, he was there physically to support Jenna.

Krista and I left the hospital so Nate and Jenna could talk. My phone rang about 8 a.m. Jenna was sobbing, saying Nate walked out of the hospital when she said she was going to keep Anna. I was secretly relieved and rejoiced in my heart. I knew Jenna didn't have it in her heart to place her child. Jenna loved children and being a mother was one of her goals and dreams.

Nate and Jenna worked through their differences and were married when Anna was eleven months old. Anna is an "apple of our eye", as is each grandchild we have. Nate and Jenna have had some very rough waters. They separated and divorced after many bitter, anger filled times and later came back together again.

Just recently Jenna shared with us an e-mail that she wrote to Nate owning her anger stemming from her own adoption and her struggle to have self-worth because of her abandonment through adoption. She shared her feelings of "not belonging" which are so common to those who are adopted. For her to begin recognizing these feelings, as her own struggle, is a huge step in healing the emotional pain she has lived with. It has been my impression that her reservoir of anger was an impenetrable wall in their marriage. The denied rejection regarding the abandonment had triggered many of Jenna's outbursts of anger in her marriage and also was a key to the struggles in our family relationships with Jenna.

Jenna completed the Mirror Images program during which she recognized her overwhelming anger issues were partially a result of her adoption abandonment. She also grew significantly through her acknowledgement and acceptance of her Korean heritage.

23

Truth from Jason

The phone rang late one night and it was Jason, our oldest son. "Mom the wedding is off! I don't know why. Heidi just said she wouldn't marry me."

The wedding was set for two weeks later and we had our airline tickets to the west coast where the ceremony was to be held in a quaint setting. Jason and Heidi had been together about one and a half years at this time.

Heidi was a lovely girl, but our hearts were still aching from the painful divorce between our son Jason and his first wife Karla. They had met at Bible College, fell in love, and married in one and a half years' time. Both were 21 years old. Karla was a beautiful Christian girl; we loved her and were so glad to have her in our family. Jason and Karla had led worship in their church. They seemed to be solid in the things of the Lord. They had the new home, new cars, the American dream, and yet it wasn't working for them.

Their marriage only lasted five years. We couldn't figure out how the marriage had gone so sour in five years' time. The complaints seemed so vague on Jason's part. He alluded to her weight; I thought Karla looked fine, not overweight at all. She was an attractive girl. Jason said, "I don't want to come home and have to be told to take out the trash."

Efforts were made to counsel, but Jason refused to engage. Karla was so confused, she called us often, prayed, counseled with her Pastors, doing all she knew how to hold things together.

I had flown out to their home to talk with Jason in person, trying to reach out to him and make sense of this decision. He was very sure he was done with the marriage, wanted no Christian help, for sure. Everything seemed so vague! We stood by and watched the marriage dissolve. We had no idea of what the *real issues* had been until this call about three years later!

Now Jason was in a second relationship that was disintegrating! Jason called us back to say he was coming home, because he had something more to tell us.

Jason is our firstborn son, overachieving, handsome, talented, and charming. He had achieved Air-Borne and Ranger status in the Army, and was a Captain by rank. We suspected alcohol had a bigger influence in his life than he wanted to admit. Living in another state made it difficult to discern what was really going on.

Terry and I worked hard at accepting Heidi, Jason's new girlfriend. We were hoping to share our faith in Christ with her at some point. Terry and I spoke with Jason and Heidi, just like we did with Chad and Sue. We expressed our grave concern about a pre-marital sexual relationship. We saw it as a setup for failure, because the relationship appeared to us to be centered on sex, distracting them from developing clear communication. We asked them to remain celibate until their marriage. They were gracious but made it clear they had made their decision and had no intention of changing their plans. So then came the engagement, and now Heidi had called off the wedding.

Jason flew home on a Friday afternoon. After dinner he sat Terry and I down in the living room. I will always remember, because we sat on the couch facing east. He sat facing us. The sun was setting and a beautiful golden glow was streaming through our bay window. Our son was sitting in this golden haze from the sunshine. The setting was so lovely, yet the words he was saying were so alarming, that the contrast in feelings is with me until today.

Jason told us that he was a sex addict. My mind went into a state of static, like buzzing in my head. He's a *what*? My son! How can this be???

Jason sobbed as he told us that he had started looking at pornography at age fourteen. He had been struggling with this addiction since then, and he was now twenty-nine years old. He told us how Heidi had found pornography on the computer and said she couldn't marry him until he got help. Jason came to tell us he knew he needed treatment, and wanted our help. Jason said he had an affair when he and Karla were married, and that's why he wasn't interested in reconciling with Karla. He still was in the throes of the addiction.

I felt an unconditional love for Jason, no judgment, just sadness and pain for him and us. He sat there broken, repenting of his sins, and asking our forgiveness for all the lies he had told us. I experienced firsthand what Father God does when we come to Him and admit we're wrong, and ask His help and forgiveness. Truly the prodigal had returned home.

Suddenly Jason's past began to make some sense. Years before when Jason was engaged to Karla, he had also dated a girl at work. When Karla found out she confronted him, he asked forgiveness, and promised to be faithful. We, along with our pastor, asked them to postpone the wedding, until as a couple they had worked through the deceit. Having talked it over, they both stated emphatically they wanted only one thing, to go ahead with the marriage.

Another puzzling thing now was clear. Karla "suspected" Jason had a drinking problem, but said he didn't drink at home. Jason also admitted to being addicted to alcohol. Also, I remembered how Karla had called saying that a lady from his office had visited Jason in the hospital after oral surgery. The lady had been wearing one of Jason's shirts! Jason's confession explained the fury with which he had responded when our youngest son Todd had earlier confronted him, about his unfaithfulness to Karla. Jason had stormed out of our home a few days before his intended birthday celebration, and had driven seven hundred miles to get away from us all! Now we understood why he wasn't eager to counsel with Karla; he was having an affair with another woman, at the time, who worked with him at the office.

Jason said he really loved Heidi and didn't want to lose her, so he was going into sexual addiction treatment. We learned of several places around the country, including a Christian treatment center. Jason refused to consider the Christian center, saying *he* would pick the place. We knew God's truth can come from many places; truth is truth. The Word of God calls Jesus the Truth.

> "I am the Way, the Truth, and the Life." John 14:6a

Jason entered a treatment center that summer. We came to join him in a "family weekend" of therapy, over July 4th that year. We only had three days with him and the counselor. I regretted there wasn't more time. The counselor explained to us, with Jason present, that most people with sexual addiction had experienced a trauma in their early life, and they coped with the pain of it in this way. She stated that Jason's trauma was being placed for adoption. At this moment Jason started to cry and tell us he could never get out of his mind why he was "given away." He had worn the mask of confidence and arrogance very well. From all outward appearances he projected someone who loved himself a lot, but here he gave voice to how he despised himself.

The counselor also asked him if he could identify any other trauma, and his response was the struggle he had when we left the

148

Catholic Church and joined a Lutheran Charismatic Church. He was thirteen at that time.

Jason shared no matter how hard he tried, he couldn't get the idea that he was "a thrown away person" out of his head. He sobbed and said, "They gave me away".

I was overcome with emotion; I cried a lot, for our son, and for myself. I ached for my son. He simply didn't feel or believe the truth of how much we loved him, and how lovable he was as a person. I wanted to take him in my arms; but that didn't happen, because he was expressing a great deal of resentment toward me at that time.

After our counseling session, Jason told how much resentment he had toward me for many things, mostly with our religious training. I listened as he shared some ways I had hurt him and I asked his forgiveness for those things. Jason also told us he had idealized Terry, and always tried to follow his example but felt like a failure.

I am so grateful for the things Jason learned about himself in treatment. He really expanded his interests, into art, opera, nature, and people. Rather than "acting out," which is the therapy term for engaging in sexual activity, he learned new ways to calm or satisfy and affirm himself. It was like getting to know a whole new person. In fact he became a different person. He told us he led a double life, because of all the lying. We were glad to meet the "real" Jason. We still feel we're learning to know him better. He has stayed in a recovery program for years, and now sponsors other addicts.

Before Jason's first marriage, the Lord gave me this verse as I prayed for Jason. I have thought of it and prayed these verses for him ever since.

"Simon, Simon Satan has asked to sift you as wheat, but I have prayed for you Simon that your faith may not fail. And when you have turned back, strengthen your brothers." Luke 22:31-32

Those hours we spent with Jason and the counselor were priceless for us as we were getting to know our son in a new way. We have watched Jason work very hard at recovery. We are proud of his efforts. This is a life long journey to replace the addiction with truth.

24

More Birth Parents

I recall the counsel we got in one of several adoption workshops. The social worker explained some possible responses the birth parent may have. She explained that the birth parent might not want to reopen the adoption chapter of their life. She made it very clear it was their prerogative, and this must be respected above all. They had signed away all rights to the child, and may never want to address the issue again. I must admit I never thought this would happen to one of our children, but it did.

Terry and I felt strongly that when we brought our children home from Family Services we became their parents. We didn't need or want any other parents in their lives. What we didn't want to face and accept was that each of our children carries part of their birth parents with them in their genes. We certainly knew this intellectually, but had not accepted this truth in our hearts. Whether we wanted it or not, the birth parents *would* be a part of our lives. This was not a problem for us as parents until the children got older. We were definitely those who believed "nurture over nature." We told them all from early on they were adopted, believing if their adoption was a natural topic for us, they would feel free to express themselves about the subject. While the children were young we talked about the fact that they grew in someone else's tummy, when we saw friends who were pregnant.

We had already experienced a variety of reactions while connecting with birth parents through our son Jason and our daughter Jenna. We now had another reunion experience. It was about seven one evening when the phone rang. Mandy called all excited, "Guess what I did today?"

"I can't guess!"

She blurted out, "I met my birth father for lunch!"

"You did what?" I was once again surprised by Mandy.

Mandy went on to say when she woke up that morning she had decided, "Today's the day I'm going to try to find Ray!" She knew from her birth mother Darlene that he had been in prison for robbery and other felonies. She pulled up the department of correction records on the Internet and found his phone number and address. She dialed him up at 10:30 a.m. and they met at noon at a local diner on the east side of town, where he lives.

Being clever as Mandy can be, she asked a friend to come along, so they could signal an exit if she was uncomfortable. She also wanted a witness and a photo of him, to study after the meeting. Mandy planned this all out, because she said she might be too nervous to really recall how he looked. She wanted to "study" his picture for similarities. I thought Mandy was wise to think of these things. Certainly the emotion of the moment could blur your perception of someone's looks.

Mandy reported Ray was really fun to visit. He too, like her birth mom, had bypass heart surgery during the past two years (Mandy had six stents in her heart at that point). Mandy said they laughed and talked a lot. She remarked that when Ray hugged her goodbye, it was her first time of "feeling loved" in her entire life. That was very hard for me to hear; seemingly negating all the love we had poured into Mandy. When I questioned her later, Mandy clarified that his hug made her feel really special, and valued by him. She craved validation, as any child would. I could totally accept that we all want to be loved and accepted in life. She had been waiting thirty-two years for this affirmation from her birth father.

Unfortunately he reported to her some very sordid details of his past, and why he was repeatedly in prison. Mandy also learned she has three half siblings from his first marriage who live on the west coast. Ray was employed at a neighborhood bar so Mandy and her hubby went to meet him there on a Friday night. Ray got into a drunken brawl, and Mandy said she never wanted to see him again. Apparently he really embarrassed her and her husband.

All these years I had prayed for her to meet these people so she could "know the truth" so the truth would set her free (John 8:32 NIV)! I idealized in my mind that she would settle down, and live more quietly once she figured out her whole story. That did not happen. This is the fifth birth parent we had some understanding of at this point, Jason's two parents, Mandy's two parents, and Jenna's mother.

Mandy's birthmother set two different dates to meet Mandy and reneged both times; Mandy's feelings of rejection by her birthmother were reinforced.

The continuing story of Jenna's contact with her birth mother had a miraculous twist after a four-year period of silence. Jenna was pregnant with Anna and delivered her in the summer. The very day she came home from the hospital with her baby, the phone rang and it was her birth mom calling from Korea. She only speaks Korean so all she said was, "Jenna, mama."

Jenna was freaked out, wondering why she would call that particular day. The amazing thing about this situation is that she did the exact same thing the day Jenna's second child, Seth, was brought home from the hospital. What are the chances of that happening? I believe it could possibly be a spiritual thing, and that Jenna's mother's spirit sensed something with Jenna, so she called. She did not call when Jenna's third child was born.

Jenna had openly expressed her anger and feelings of abandonment. I accepted those feelings as legitimate. Jenna has been abandoned by both parents. As time passed I spoke with Jenna about having mercy on her birth mom. After having a child of her own, I felt Jenna would now be more understanding. I was also remembering the letter sent from the agency along with Jenna's mother's contact letter that indicated the mother herself had been an orphan. The letter indicated a great amount of anguish about her past decision to place Jenna. I asked Jenna to consider forgiving and releasing her mom.

Jenna finally did write her own letter, and sent photos of her children to the birth mother. She sent the letter through the Christian adoption Agency. Jenna has since e-mailed with her birth sisters regarding medical history. Now Jenna has had some Facebook relationship with one of her birth sisters.

My two Korean sons, Chad and Todd, would like to hear from their birth families. I pray God will allow them to hear someday. I now realize God knows all sides of the situation, and He knows what the right time is for each child.

During development in the womb a child learns to recognize the sound of parental voices, to know the heartbeat of the mother. A new different caregiver, even if from the day of birth will not be the same. A sense of abandonment will be present when those caregivers are not those remembered from the womb.

The wound resulting from the cutting away from the biological family must be addressed. The in-grafting into the trunk of the new family tree must allow the nurturing sap to flow into the branch, for strength and new growth to develop.

I remember that I contacted Mandy's mother Darlene myself as we were struggling with Mandy and were looking for some answers. I requested that we meet to talk. Darlene surprised me as she readily agreed to meet with me. I wondered if she would even show up. I told her, "My own blood family has had lots of problems. I only want to learn some of Mandy's family history that could possibly help us better love and understand our daughter."

Darlene did show up at our agreed upon meeting place, a fast food restaurant on the east side of town located just two miles away from where Terry had grown up. I had read the agency's description of Darlene as a large unkempt looking woman. I watched the door, waiting for her to come in late.

Right on time, a pleasant looking well-kept full-figured woman, about the same age as me came walking in. It wasn't hard to find each other, for we were the only ones there! I found Darlene to be friendly and attractive. As she sat down, I began to explain my reason for wanting to meet her. We had many challenges with Mandy, and were hoping to make some sense of it through her family history. I repeated my statement that I had many dysfunctional issues in my own family of origin, and I didn't want her to feel that I thought myself better than her.

We learned both of us had attended Al-anon because of family drinking problems, both because of our daughters. We felt connected as we compared notes on my raising Mandy and her raising her older daughter Dawn, as we saw many similarities. One difference is that

Mandy had not wound up in juvenile court, whereas her daughter Dawn had been in the court system since age fourteen, and quit school at age sixteen.

I was starting to feel more successful already. (Having just read what I wrote here is interesting to me. To say I felt "successful" is odd, I think! Why that word? Why not relieved? Was there some inner sense I had to prove I was a good mother? Maybe so!) We commiserated on the challenges of parenting, and actually laughed a lot, probably a nervous laughter. We decided that, under other circumstances, we could have become friends. We thought alike on many issues.

I couldn't help notice her lovely long fingernails. Mandy loves getting manicures and has the same graceful hands. Also Darlene said she loved to wear wigs, which is another thing Mandy likes to do. There is flamboyance about Mandy similar to how Darlene described herself.

I asked Darlene why she never pursued a relationship with Mandy. She explained that Mandy took her "so off guard" by coming to her work place, in a retail store, introducing herself. She described that she had been speechless and hadn't known what to say!

Darlene said Mandy's first words to her were, "I hope you're not prejudiced against blacks. Are you?"

Darlene seemed to disconnect emotionally from our discussion at this point, which is similar to how Mandy has disconnected in our difficult discussions. This was all too familiar for me.

Darlene explained the circumstances of Mandy's birth. She already had a one-year-old daughter. She had lived at her parent's home with her first child during the entire second pregnancy. She kept her pregnancy a secret from her father. She said her dad died, never knowing about Mandy's existence. Her mom forced her to place Mandy for adoption. Darlene was already raising one child alone, two years older than Mandy, and couldn't care for two. I felt sad for Mandy, in utero, being held a captive of secrecy, and shame. No wonder Mandy often felt anxious and rejected, as this had begun for her in the womb.

Darlene explained she could not bring herself to sign the final adoption papers. That was why Mandy had been in foster care for three months before being released for adoption. Darlene said the birth father was "a complete a—hole" whom she hated. She wanted no part of him, and wanted to keep that chapter of her life closed. She also said her mom had died close to the time Mandy came to meet her in the store. Darlene had not been able to "deal with" meeting Mandy and all the issues of her adoption along with her grief at her own mother's death.

Darlene married two years after having Mandy, and was still married to the same man. She had another child, a boy, with her husband. She had been employed by the same employer the last twenty years, and enjoyed her work. I left this meeting comforted to know she also had trouble with her own daughter, not that I wished trouble on anyone. I couldn't help wondering if both of Darlene's daughters had the same father because our file said she had dated the man for several years. Both girls seemed to have major social struggles, which suggested to me they could be biological siblings.

Darlene seemed stable and normal, having worked at the same job and being married to the same man for over twenty years. The meeting gave me hope that Mandy would someday move beyond her choices of wild living.

I pushed my way through for Mandy to know more about her birth mother, and nothing really beneficial came from it, except more rejection for Mandy. It's another case of my not "letting go", and allowing God to be God in my family's lives!

> "For My thoughts are not your thoughts, neither are your ways My ways, declares the Lord. As the heavens are higher than the earth, so are My ways higher than your ways and My thoughts than your thoughts." Isaiah 55:8-9

When Mandy was twenty-nine, several years after I met Darlene, Mandy had a heart attack. I called Darlene to tell her and ask if there was a history of heart trouble in their family. "Oh yes," she replied, "I had a triple bypass at age forty!" Her parting words were, "Tell Mandy we love her!"

I got off the phone, feeling my blood pressure rising. I thought, "Why don't you tell her yourself!" I surprised myself at my strong angry response. It was anger over Darlene's continued rejection of Mandy. I hurt for my child who needed to hear from this birth mom, some words of affirmation. But I had been warned by the adoption agency that it might go this way; it was the risk of agreeing to be a part of the adoption triad. During one of the many counseling sessions we had through the years, the counselor used the word "idealist" to describe me. I had considered myself an idealist and thought it was a good thing. But when I looked up the word "idealism" in the Webster dictionary it said; "behavior or thought based on a conception of things as they should be or as one would wish them to be." Next the word "idealist" is described as "a person whose behavior or thought is based on ideals; often used contemptuously to mean an impractical visionary or dreamer."

Whoa, I didn't like reading the thought that I could be considered foolish for the high standards which I placed on myself and everyone else! Ouch, that hurt, but I admit I found it to be true. In my idealistic worldview, these birth parents would embrace the children, all would forgive one another, all the birth parents would like us, and we'd all live happily ever after!

There were many disillusioning things that occurred during the birth parent encounters. I have decided to leave it in God's hands as to what He wants for our two sons, regarding finding their birth parents. (As if I *really* had any power!)

We have prayed for all ten biological parents, who have given us the best gift of all: our precious family, our children. If it weren't for their decisions to give up their children, we wouldn't have had the awesome privilege of parenting our family or have our sweet grandchildren! We are indebted to them and we pray blessings into their lives on a regular basis!

25

Letting Go

Terry and I were juggling the relationship challenges regarding the birth parents of our children while still in the midst of raising Mandy's children in our home. Here I was again. I felt I was in the same emotional place I had been in twenty-five years earlier. Depleted! I had nothing left to give. Being a Christian, or not, I could not drum up enough enthusiasm for life to be free of the troubles all around. I felt if I loved enough, everyone would be all right. I knew I didn't *love* the way I wanted to! I thought *love* for these children would be enough. It wasn't. The challenges of continuous daily care for everyone seemed to be too much for me.

Josie was under the illusion that she could fix her children and their emotional pain by loving them. She firmly believed that with "God all things are possible." When was God going to fix things the way she thought they should be? God does not always work our lives the way we think they should go. He has an eternal plan bigger and better than anything we can imagine. That is why we must "walk in faith and not sight". We must trust Him in everything, knowing He is working for the eternal good of everyone under His care. Many times an individual needs to come to the place of no other choices than asking for God's help, rather than expecting people to take care of our needs and wants. Parents may be interfering with God's plan by fixing and manipulating their children's dilemmas. We need to Thank and Trust God when we don't understand what is happening. He is

Sovereign and a Mighty God who has promised His children, "He will never leave us or forsake us." This is perhaps the biggest problem for most Christians who want to have life follow in their own plans, rather than trusting God to allow the challenges and hard places which bring individuals to a place where they need a Savior, not a mother or father.

Basically I am a joyful person; but, after four and a half years of raising the granddaughters, and dealing with the other crises of the other children, I was anything but joyful. I felt like I was trudging through life, feeling defeated, frequently emotionally spent.

We spoke to the school psychologist about the possibility of placing the girls in a foster home. She said this was not an option; the county would not pay for foster care because we had custody! We asked if one of the girls could be placed, with us still maintaining weekly contact. Their answer was a resounding no, the girls needed to be together. Our experience was that the two together drew from us emotionally more than we felt able to give. The girls seemed to "play" off each other and seemed to enjoy triggering each other into escalating behaviors!

Krista, our foster daughter, felt strongly that the girls needed Mandy. She suggested we try to engage Mandy back into Tyesha and Jewel's lives as they may need assurance of their mother's love. (Remember, Krista was orphaned at 11 years old.) I was scared "out of my mind" and resisted the idea, thinking we would be trapped into the old cycle once again. Then I decided my fear was not "of the Lord," so began to consider Krista's idea. Krista invited Mandy to her home during the school year the girls lived with Krista.

By this time Mandy had been more involved with her daughters, visiting regularly, buying them clothes, and showing interest in their

161

lives. We spoke to her about the court stipulations for the girls return. There were three specific requirements:

1) Counseling on parenting for her and any man in her home

2) Consecutive supervised visits

3) Random drug tests

Mandy decided to take action to work towards getting her daughters back into her home. Mandy made the necessary arrangements for supervised visitation and submitted to random drug tests. We were guarded, but hopeful that she would be successful.

Mandy passed the random drug tests and both she and James had been free of violations with the law for six months as per the court order. We also requested Mandy and James to do some family training on parenting after their marriage. Now married, Mandy and James arranged for family counseling at a Christian agency. James thought parenting was going to be "fun." He concluded, "You have to be a playmate to the kids and they'll be fine."

After Mandy and James completed the parenting classes, we did release the girls one at a time. We decided on a plan for separate entry for each girl which seemed to be a good plan for each girl to have time alone to adjust to their mom and their new living arrangements. I was optimistically cautious because we had seen more cooperation and change in Mandy during that past year than many previous years combined.

We sent Tyesha home to live with her mom and new stepdad during Christmas break. She had lived with us four and a half years but returned gleefully to her home and it seemed to go well. Tyesha went to school regularly and was happy to be home with mom.

We kept Jewel six more months, thinking Mandy could ease into parenting and adjust to parenting one girl at a time. This arrangement seemed to be good for the girls, too.

The day Jewel left our home was a day of very mixed emotions for me. I was glad Mandy had finally stepped up to her responsibilities, but also was sad to see Jewel skipping out the door. She stood on the landing, waved goodbye and off she went, with no apparent sadness at all. I needed or should I say I "wanted," some hugs, some tears, some sign of sadness leaving us; but she was just excited about returning to her "family." Admittedly, my mixed emotions probably included a great sigh of relief, glad to be free of the daily care. My emotions were totally torn between relief and anxiety for the future of the girls' lives. Would Mandy take hold and be a responsible parent? Was her change sincere? I was fearful about giving the control of my granddaughters into their mother's hands.

We had kept our grandchildren five years. Tyesha was now 10 and Jewel was 8 ½ when they went home again to live with their mother.

Terry had retired in early spring of that year. The girls went back to live in their mother's home, and one month later Terry and I left for China, ready to go on with our own lives. Terry had agreed to take a six-month missionary work assignment in China, which would allow a missionary family to take a leave of absence back to the states.

Terry and I had lived in our home 33 years. We talked about moving at various times but we never reached the point of wanting to do so at the same time. Terry had always dreamed of building a home on a wooded lot so we kept looking around at what was available. We found the perfect lot and agreed to purchase it, our first step to eventually building our new home. We then bought the lot, picked the contractor and had the house designed. Everything was put on hold for our six-month trip to China.

Hindsight is always clear. It wasn't until Jewel was fourteen that she revealed to us how very quickly her excitement had turned to sadness after she got back home. Jewel told us her mom started to drink again within the first month.

We had been the girls' safety net but this time we were far away in China. After we returned from China we had more time with the girls and discovered Mandy was back to doing her own thing and this time the girls were adjusted to doing their own thing, too. They were running with the freedom of a non-attentive parent and engaging in acting out behaviors of truancy, breaking curfew and fighting in school. When we became aware of what was happening we offered the option of a foster home for Jewel with her former Sunday school teacher. We took her to visit their home and arrangements were made for her to move in on Friday. The family rearranged their home to accommodate her. The day before she was to move in, she called, "I changed my mind. I have to stay home to take care of my mom."

I knew the pull for acceptance from her natural mother was very strong. Both granddaughters wanted to be near their mom. We became aware of the fact they had unsupervised freedom to do what would never have been allowed under Grandma's care. The truth was the girls did not have to choose illegal behaviors. We had tried to offer supervised living. They could have asked for help and would have been heard. They made their own choices, which had inevitable consequences.

About this same time we found out Peanut, the girls' father, was back in prison. I called Prison Fellowship again, and asked them to contact him, because I know our Father God is looking for every lost sheep! Another interesting twist to the story was that Peanut's father, who taught him how to pimp, was in a new marriage. This was another example of God's amazing hand moving in people's lives. Peanut's father had divorced Peanut's step mom, had married again and had become a father again at the age of 48.

When we returned Tyesha and Jewel to Mandy, I felt the Lord say that *I should not* take them to Church on Sunday. Wow! Why would God say that? I obeyed, mostly because I was too emotionally exhausted to do anything else. At this time, Terry and I were focusing on our own emotional and spiritual health, and that of our son Todd.

One day Tyesha told me how much she loved *"her new church!"* My ears perked up, and I asked where she went. Tyesha explained a bus picked up her, Jewel and their friend and took them to a Baptist church in a neighboring community. I was delighted to hear they were attending and now knew why I had been told not to go pick them up for church each Sunday. Tyesha smiled, knowing I would be pleased. "We are being water baptized and want you and Grampa to be there!" Of course we would not miss that occasion!

After the church service I went downstairs to thank the girls' bus driver for his faithful service. Jewel grabbed me and pulled my arm. "I want you to meet our other Grandma!"

I thought, "What? Other grandmother? Who?"

The lady was Peanut's dad's new wife.

The girls introduced me to Rachel who now was the girl's "step grandma."

Rachel told me, "I am a brand new four-month-old Christian. And, I am working on their grandpa (Rod) to come to church with me!"

I told her, "We have been praying for him for a long time!"

"Great! I know that it is just a matter of time before he comes with me!"

How amazing is that story? Only God could arrange this.

The next year, I had a most remarkable reunion with Peanut's dad at his Afro-American Baptist church. Terry and I took Tyesha and Jewel to their grandfather's church because they told us he had become a Christian. The girls told us it was a very "energetic" church. That was an understatement.

We arrived late at 11:10 for a 10:45 service. Ushers uniformed in classy robes and white gloves blocked us from entering before the appropriate time in the service for late arrivals. The ushers were poised and impressive. At the right time, we were quickly marched to the front row of a packed church. Terry and I were the white minority. The place was rocking and swaying and praising God with an enthusiasm that blessed me through and through. Ladies were dressed in lovely dresses, white gloves, beautiful wide brimmed hats; the men had on suits, the little girls were dressed in their finest. Everyone sang, and the preacher preached, then they sang some more, and he preached some more. I knew I had been to church.

After the service ended we visited Peanut's dad, his wife and their child outside on the boulevard on this lovely sunny day. Peanut's dad had on a powder blue suit, silver tie, wide brimmed blue hat, and a huge gold cross hanging around his neck. Impulsively I grabbed the cross in my enthusiasm, and said, "I never thought I'd see this day."

He smiled into my eyes. "Why not Josie? Didn't I ever tell you my daddy was a gospel singer? I was just a rebellious young man!"

I asked if he remembered our visit 17 years earlier, when his son and my daughter were talking marriage after only having known each other three months.

He said, "Yes I do. Chi Chi's Restaurant, right?"

166

This day was an answer to many prayers. I thanked God for drawing Rod to faith. I was ecstatic, thinking of God's amazing grace, always calling His children to Himself. Once again the words from Isaiah rang in my mind.

> "My thoughts are not your thoughts, neither are your ways
> My ways, declares the Lord. As the heavens are higher
> than the earth, so are My ways higher than your ways, and
> My thoughts than your thoughts." Isaiah 55:8-9

The irony of this conversation is that I wound up encouraging him about his son, Peanut. Rod exclaimed, "Yah, well he's back in prison again. He'll never change!"

I quickly responded, not missing an opportunity, "I know there will be a day, just like with you! I know someday Peanut will also walk with the Lord. I know it in my heart!"

That same summer Rod's little girl was in my group at an inner city vacation bible school. She ran up to me, hugging me, saying, "We're related! Sorta'!"

One of those, "Well, huh…moments."

> "This is the confidence we have in approaching God:
> that if We ask anything according to His will He
> hears us." 1 John 5:14

The Word of God says, if we pray, believing, it is always God's will to save and deliver His people, as He did with Peanut's dad.

Therein is the dilemma of walking by faith. When God speaks something to our heart for ourselves or for someone we are praying for, but the present natural circumstances are very different, in faith, trust God to work out the situation in His way, in His time!

When I was a new believer, answers came quickly on many things. It was God's way of building my trust in Him. Now over thirty years have passed and I am still praying on some requests. I know God is continuing to do His part to draw those I love to faith, but He will never force Himself on anyone. I am so glad He never forced me. I can ask no less as He deals with those I love.

26

The Battle Against Cancer

After returning home from China, we decided to begin the construction of our new home. In the midst of the construction, my dad was diagnosed with cancer and was hospitalized. This was a very stressful time for me with all the construction decisions and my father's rapidly deteriorating health. My father, 94½, died within two weeks of being diagnosed with pancreatic cancer. We built the home handicap accessible so dad could visit, but he never lived to enjoy it with us.

One year after moving into our new home, we had a guest from China. While living in China we had invited her to come to the U.S. for a Christian conference desiring for her to experience both the freedom of worship we have in the U.S. and the gathering of international Christian women. Women came from 163 nations to that International conference for four days, to hear from the Lord through anointed leaders. We had a wonderful time together and I knew she was experiencing and enjoying free worship for the first time in her life.

I remember thinking I was the happiest I had ever been, full of joy, and satisfied with where I was in life. While I was at this conference I first noticed the red rash like mark on my right breast. When we got home, my friend returned to China, and I made an appointment with my gynecologist to check out the mark. The doctor was sure it was nothing and put me on antibiotics for one week. The spot didn't change, so she immediately sent me for a mammogram, which led to a biopsy. The biopsy came back positive for cancer.

I went to a prayer meeting the day we were waiting for the results. I had decided to go the prayer meeting rather than wait agonizing by the phone. When I came back home and walked in the door, I could tell Terry was really upset. He blurted out, with a cracking voice and tears in his eyes, "The doctor called and its cancer!"

While we held each other tight I felt an inner strength and resolve straight from God. My thought was, "God is Sovereign! He allowed this for a reason. I will be alright." Now in retrospect I know this assurance was all His grace. If I had any clue of all I was going to go through in the next months I probably would have fainted on the spot.

This was just two years after the girls had gone back to live with their Mom. We could see the girls' lives with their mom were still in great upheaval. We offered both girls placement in Christian homes, but both girls declined, choosing to "be home" with mom. At this time, they felt they were protecting her, as they watched the choices she made.

We thought about bringing the girls back again into our home, but because of my diagnosis of breast cancer we had to let them face both the consequences of their own behaviors and their mother's behaviors.

Now, Jewel, our fourteen-year-old granddaughter, was struggling with depression and cutting, and was in the hospital for psychiatric treatment. Mandy demonstrated a mother's heart when she called crying, "I wish I could help my daughter some way."

I said, "You can. You can tell her the truth of why they lived with us."

"But I can't, I don't know what to say."

I said, "Tell you what. Why don't you practice by saying to me what you think you should say to Jewel."

"OK." She began cautiously, "I was not ready to be a mom, and I didn't want the responsibility. I just didn't know how to be a mom".

I said, "That is good. She'll get it and be so glad you finally speak the truth to her."

Prior to this time the girls would try to talk with Mandy about those five years away from her and she would change the subject or say, "Let's not talk about this now."

God was bringing healing to Jewel's heart, again not when or how I wanted it. I praised God that He was sovereignly directing the situation for the truth to be finally told to the Jewel and her sister.

I now had to begin a long journey of physical healing. I was diagnosed with Inflammatory Breast Cancer, Stage 3 (with lymph node involvement). This is a cancer which is very often terminal. The cancer treatment lasted for one year during which time many people were God's hands and feet for Terry and me. Everything stopped to focus on my getting well. I had a lumpectomy, eight rounds of chemo, a mastectomy, reconstruction surgery, and 28 radiation treatments. The scripture was a constant source of comfort and direction. Terry was remarkable in his strength and support for me. When I lost my hair during the first round of chemo he shaved his head. I'll never forget when he walked in the house, on a very cold January day, bald as a cucumber, grinning from ear to ear.

I screamed, "What did you do?"

Terry grinned like a twelve year old, and said, "We're going through this together!" In my mind, that was the most romantic thing he had ever done for me. He slept with a hat on to keep his head warm!

My dear friend Sandy had conquered cancer five years earlier and sent me a little note sharing some verses from Psalm 27 that had really helped her stay focused during her grueling treatments. I read these repeatedly to comfort and to calm my fears.

> "The Lord is my light and my Salvation, whom shall I fear? The Lord is the Stronghold of my life, of whom I shall be afraid... Though an army besieges me my heart will not fear; though war breaks out against me, even then I will be confident... For in the day of trouble He will keep me safe in His dwelling...I am still confident of this; I will see the goodness of the Lord in the land of the living. Wait for the Lord; be strong and take heart and wait for the Lord." Psalm 27:1, 3, 5a, 13-14

Terry and I repeated these words together many times during chemo.

During this time, I also had to get a test for my heart. I sat in a waiting room in a Catholic hospital. A man walking by placed a tract in my hand. Once again it was Psalm 27! God really wanted me to know He had me in His hands, caring for me.

During the cancer treatments, I learned from my cancer support group that I would need all the energy I had, to recover. They suggested we list all our friends and relatives in two groups: those who brought energy to me and those who took energy from me. They suggested I avoid any contact with those who drained my energy. I knew I needed personal counseling to learn how to "release" my worries about my children to the Lord. I knew I needed to learn how to let go, that it was not necessary for me to "carry" my children's burdens. All of my children blessed me mightily by agreeing to go with me to the counselor.

My biggest heartache at that time was the nonexistent relationship with our son Chad. The counselor helped me stop "beating my head against the wall," in attempts to mend the broken relationship with our son Chad. Her words were, "It is what it is!"

This was very freeing for me, to learn that we can only have relationship with those who want to relate with us and only to the depth that they want. The counselor told me the very poignant story of Judas in "The Passion" movie, by Mel Gibson. She pointed out that we don't see Jesus begging Judas to come back. God gives each of us a free will and lets us do what we want until we choose to come to Him. That illustration was very clear for me and impacted me deeply as a principle for all relationships. Even Jesus Christ, the perfect man, struggled and was rejected by those close to Him. Jesus was not standing by begging Judas to change his mind, but let him go!

I had to accept that Jesus puts His hand out to us, and we are free to accept it. If we don't, he allows us our freedom to reject Him and He goes on with those willing to be with Him. This has helped me channel my feelings into trust, and patience, waiting on Chad to decide whether or not he wants us as parents and/or friends in his life.

Brennan Manning (2002) states, "…trust is the courage to accept acceptance" (p.102). It means that I can lean into God's character of Hesed (Hebrew for "loving kindness"). Trust means I believe God is Sovereign, in charge of my life and has my good in His heart at all times. The sovereignty of God has been my biggest comfort throughout life. God is a Father I can trust.

"God is not a man that he should lie, nor a son of man that He should change His mind." Numbers 23:19a

By meditating on this idea of acceptance, my trust in God grew knowing that God cares for Chad more than we do. God is Chad's Father! He will move toward Chad the moment Chad moves towards Him. Until Chad wants something different in his relationship with us, I repeat, "It is what it is!"

I needed to stop trying to manipulate the relationship into what I wanted. How ludicrous this is as if I had any power over any person except myself. I can only control how and when and who I relate with. And sometimes I admit I don't do very well controlling myself.

How freeing it is to "not expect," but only to be thankful for whatever communication there is. No more "going after" Chad, trying to convince him of my love!

We watched Chad run himself ragged, bouncing all these balls, trying to keep up visitation with his two families, while appearing to be dying inside. We have spoken to him about self-hate, unforgiveness of himself, and all he holds against others and us. His only response is that it is too hard to forgive. Chad had told me I had failed him as a mom. I knew I could have done better so asked his forgiveness. The Mirror Images program has helped me reach out to Chad with truth about our relationship through the reconciliation process using letters to help us communicate.

Our counselor said Chad needed to choose whether or not to engage in life. We should pray for him to have the courage to face himself and his own life! Her thought was that he might live out his days a very lonely man, if he does not choose a new way.

We keep our eyes on Father God, knowing He is there to help Chad, when Chad is ready. It has been years since Chad considered treatment. He has a job, has moved from a room to a house he rents, and he visits his kids regularly. He says he's happy and this is all he wants and needs.

About two months after the session with the counselor, we learned that Chad was using hard drugs. We went to a chemical dependency counselor to prepare to do an intervention. The very next day Chad came asking us for help because he was scared for himself! We gave him numbers to call for help and offered to pay half the cost of treatment. He investigated these facilities, but declined the options, refusing to accept responsibility for half the cost of treatment, saying he would not take on more debt.

During our encounter with Chad, we relied heavily on Jason, our older son, who had been through treatment. Jason said Chad didn't need to go inpatient, if he chose not to. He could still work and go to nightly AA meetings. Chad did go to meetings, several times, to our knowledge.

My counselor had helped me to separate from my "adult children" by owning my own stuff, and letting them own their own problems! The struggles with my parenting have shown me how unforgiveness is an impenetrable wall that holds us prisoner, until one party is willing to forgive and release the other. One twelve-step definition of unforgiveness is "Taking poison and hoping the other person gets sick." Unforgiveness hurts you, and does not hurt the other person at all.

The biggest lesson I learned from the cancer was how much God and others loved me. I was totally overwhelmed by the outpouring of love, cards, flowers, and meals that came our way. Our children were so tender and concerned for me. It was hard for me to see them suffer and be fearful for me. One of my personal beliefs was "I never wanted to cause anyone any trouble!" I learned I needed to graciously receive love as well as to be able to give love. I deny others an opportunity to love if I don't let them help me. I gave freely to others, but had a hard time receiving myself. Learning how to be a gracious receiver seemed to be part of my assignment. All the acts of love became a gift for me to help me enjoy life so much more, and to be gentler with myself. I had to set aside being "Mom" for the moment, to stop worrying about everyone else, and just take care of myself.

We learned the necessity of asking for and accepting help of many different kinds. We always brought friends with us to the five-hour chemo sessions. We used it as a visiting and prayer time, calling on God for healing. A hard stressful time became very palatable as we spent this quality time with those close to us. Both Terry and I learned the huge lesson about the importance of leaning on others in the body of Christ for comfort and strength when ours was failing.

Another thing I learned was how replaceable I am. Everything went on fine without me; at church, at home, everywhere. I really believe God was speaking loud and clear to me to slow down the pace of my life, spend more time with Him, and just be quiet. Since that time, I try to only schedule one major thing a day, because peace has become a very important personal value I'm trying to cultivate. The Bible calls Christ the "Prince of Peace."

I also learned about setting daily priorities for my life. So many times certain projects seemed urgent. When my life was on the line, nothing was urgent, other than having good relationships with God, my family and those I loved.

Another thing I learned in the cancer support group Terry and I went to was that cancer was the "twisted gift." The facilitator meant that the cancer could become a teacher to lead us to a more deliberate life. God states the same thing in the Bible when Joseph identified himself to his brothers who betrayed him and sold him into slavery in Egypt. At that time he is ruler over all Egypt, and is reunited with his brothers, because of a famine in their land. They are afraid for their lives, because of his possible retribution. Joseph tells them not to fear, God had a bigger plan.

> "You intended to harm me, but God intended it for good to accomplish what is now being done, the saving of many lives." Genesis 50:20
>
> The Living Bible says, "As far as I am concerned, God turned into good what you meant for evil."

I realize my cancer brought pain to my family and me, but God used it to bring healing and blessings to me also. I believe I am a better person today with more trust and understanding of who God is, because of this journey. God was faithful to me beyond measure in every small detail. He comforted me as I lay in pain too sick to move. He became my all and all. He was more than enough for me. He was sufficient. Life became very simple and uncomplicated and I could see Him more clearly, He was my focus.

I still appreciate each day more than I had before, the colors of nature around me are brighter, the stars are shinier, and my family means more to me than ever before because I had to face the possibility of my death and the eternity beyond.

My family has grown through it, and I grab hold of life in a much firmer way, because of it, determined to fulfill God's calling on my life. The book of Job in the Bible includes a portion about adversity that stuck with me during this trial.

> "Though He slay me, YET will I hope in Him." Job 13:15

Job was tormented, physically with boils and emotionally by his friends, yet he chose to stand with the knowledge that God was trustworthy. I took the same resolve and God did not disappoint me.

While in the battle against cancer, our pastor prayed with me during our Sunday worship time. As he laid his hands on me I fell to the floor under the power of God. The power of God surged through my entire body, feeling like sound waves, moving over me. I knew God was touching me. At the very same time, six hundred miles away, a dear friend was praying for me. She said God spoke to her heart and said He was going to touch me with His glory. As we talked later in the day we realized this had happened at exactly the same time, in two separate places. Praise God for His healing power.

During my battle with cancer, Mandy did something dear and sweet for me that knit us together in a special way. Terry and I were scheduled to go to Poland on a mission trip with our church. My doctors assured me I would be well enough by summer to go, but as time came closer, I was still involved with reconstruction surgery following the mastectomy. Surgery was scheduled at the time we had plans to leave for Poland. Terry and I decided he would go ahead with the team, and I would stay home to recover from surgery. Since I'd just be resting anyway, I wanted him to go ahead with the team. The only problem was that I needed my extensive dressings changed each morning. I planned to call a nurse friend for help but Mandy insisted she would come daily to change my bandages. I was thankful for her willingness and received her offer. Mandy showed up every day for two weeks between seven and seven thirty a.m. to change my bandages. It was a very personal and intimate time for us both. I was cut from one side of my chest to the other. Mandy handled this job with cheer and humor. As she stood next to me in our bathroom, applying crème to my wounds with a q-tip, I marveled at this scene in the mirror. Mandy and I have had many struggles but now I was thanking God for her devoted help. Truly God is able to do amazing things, changing our hearts and bonding us in a way I never would have imagined.

27

Father Knows Best

God has a way of giving us gifts even when we don't ask for them! He gives us gifts He knows we need, giving them in His time and His way. One of God's greatest gifts to me is when He orchestrates an emotional healing that He knows I need, even if I am not aware of my need. These unplanned "surprise" experiences are as valuable as gold, always strengthening my character, and my spiritual resolve making me a more stable Christian.

On a lovely fall day Terry and I drove to Whitefish Montana for my nephew's wedding. The gala event was held on a ski slope surrounded by the majestic Rocky Mountains. My nephew was obviously "head over heels" in love with his fiancé, so joining them at their wedding was a special treat for us. After the reception and gift opening we drove west on a sightseeing ride to the top of the area's highest mountain to soak in the awesome majesty of this part of God's creation. It seemed like God was "showing off" when He created this part of the country!

Our son Jason had lived near this mountain the first years of his marriage to Karla. Their divorce after six years of marriage had always been a confusing puzzling time for us. Jason and Karla began their marriage as an "enthusiastic young Christian couple." Jason and Karla looked like the model Christian couple. We had expected them to pray through the hurdles of their marriage, get Godly counsel, and live happily ever after! But the reality of their life together was far different than our expectations.

Now ten years later after the divorce from his first wife Karla, Jason had asked us to stop by his old house and take a picture for him. We located the house, and took some photos. The neighborhood looked more than ten years old with faded fences and worn curbs. Terry had helped Jason plant trees, which were now grown, almost hiding the house. The area had been a new development when Jason and Karla moved in. In some ways I felt like my life and heart were as worn as much as the neighborhood looked. There had been so much pain in those ten years. Jason had divorced Karla, had another relationship, and now was filing for his second divorce. What we didn't know at the time of the first divorce was that Jason was in the throes of sexual addiction, and leading a double life.

Now as we sat there in front of that home with some of the answers, memories of the last ten years came flooding over me. I began to cry, suddenly flooded with emotions from all the emotional pain we had walked through during those ten years. All this "history" and the unanswered questions to which we now had answers, overwhelmed me as we sat there staring at the house where Jason had lived. Now I was sobbing. I was washed over with grief. Looking at the house triggered my deep emotional response from the painful consequences of Jason's choices. I was surprised at the amount of my grief that I had not been aware of, yet had carried through these years. As I wept I had a deeper healing of my emotions God knew I needed.

We were startled because Jason called us at that very moment as we sat near his old house. He could hear from my voice that I had been crying. I told him about the pain and sorrow I was experiencing from the memories of our losses. He replied that he was sorry and that it had been a very shame filled time of his life. He said he had many regrets and again said he was sorry for hurting us.

We also asked for and received Jason's forgiveness for our part in his struggle. There are consequences from sin, which follow us. It has been heart wrenching for us to see Jason struggle to love and accept himself. He struggles to avoid the addictions of both sex and alcohol. Jason lost everything in the first divorce: wife, home, dog, car, and the faith he had. But God has promised me that Jason would serve Him again someday.

Jason is still in SLAA (Sex and Love Addicts Anonymous). He has been a lead speaker, has sponsored others, and has learned a lot. We watched him mature. He is now able to express his feelings, reflect on his behaviors and works to live by the 12-step program, which is a method of walking the Christian faith.

I began to reflect on what could have been done differently while raising him to help him avoid this painful path. The one area I really felt lacking in my own heart and life was the ability to "nurture" my children. All my friends say I am a great encourager and exhorter; however, I personally feel I have fallen short with my own family.

I couldn't help but thank our God and Father for His help during those tumultuous confusing times. I know God brought us through our many troubled times and we all are stronger because of it. One of the miracles of understanding was brought to us through a broadcast of "Oprah." Yes, Oprah had a special on sexual addictions the very week Jason confessed to us what his troubles were. The show had been taped for us. Oprah interviewed many former sex addicts which helped me begin to understand the root of what we were dealing with, and definitely helped take away some of the shame. Most of the people have some secret deep hurt during their childhood. The sexual satisfaction is used to cover, numb or deny the pain at first, but then addiction overtakes them. The double life triggers shame, which the addictive person tends to anesthetize with more of the addictive behavior. This is the downward spiral. Statistics say that 3-5% of the population struggles with sexual addiction (Brandt, K., 2009). At least our son was getting the help he desperately needed. Jason recommended books to help us understand. (See Resources)

As we sat in front of Jason's former house the healing miracle was the release of the grief I didn't even know was still there, residing in my spirit and emotions. I believe many people are walking around wounded and grieving, and they don't know it is there, until something "triggers" the grief for them. I was grateful for this encounter and release, which I feel God orchestrated.

I often pray for God to reveal any area in my life where I still need healing. God set up this situation to heal me, much to my surprise. As we walk through the grief, the traumatic memories lose their grip and God can begin to heal our emotions.

I believe grieving is a core issue for adopted adults, but most of them haven't been able to put into words the strong unidentified feelings they have. Webster's New World Dictionary describes the word "grief" as "intense emotional suffering caused by loss, acute sorrow and deep sadness."

Adoptive parents may also have to grieve their lost dreams for their lives and their children, when things go differently than they had planned. When both adoptive parents and adopted children heal from their personal grief, they will be free to love and be loved with no walls between them. Terry and my expectations were a fantasy from our dreams of what a happy family should look like. Our responsibility as parents is to examine our expectations, dismantling them and replacing them with truth.

Those who have been birth parents and who have given up children for adoption to others also have to acknowledge their own personal loss and grief.

God wants us free to worship Him and enjoy the life He has given us. If we have stuffed and denied emotional pain we are not able to fully love God, our family members or ourselves. To love one another is our "high calling" from God. Only as we are emotionally freed can we minister that love and freedom to family and then on to others.

> "Then you will know the truth and the truth will set you free!" John 8:32

Adoptive parents and adoptees that acknowledge and grieve their individual losses are able to love freely and without reservation.

28

Facing My Own Issues

I was almost forty years old before I acknowledged my own pain and need for nurture. I took Elijah House Ministries Prayer Counselor training. John Sanford's "Inner Healing of the Wounds of the Heart" was part of our ministry training. I participated in small group work, agreeing to accept feedback from the other trainees.

I told the group about my mother's continuous statements of only wanting to have one child and that I had decided I never wanted to be like my mother. The people in the group had identified bitterness and disappointment from me as I told my story. The class suggested I needed to forgive my parents. My statements had been seen as judgments, which they believed had affected my life. They led me in prayer to forgive my parents for not nurturing me the way I had wanted, needed or *expected*. I chose to purposely forgive my mom for saying she only wanted one child. I chose to tell myself I was intended to be and that I was not a burden by being alive. I chose to accept the truth that God intended for me to be born, and that I wasn't a mistake, that I had a right to be here on this earth. I had to choose to believe the words from Revelation:

> "For You have created all things and for Your pleasure they were created." Revelation 4:11b

I choose to believe I give God pleasure, that He created me to have friendship with Him, and that He wants me on this earth.

When I understood this and prayed, I felt a new joy in my heart. I trust the same freedom will happen for any adopted person who asks God to heal those feelings of not being wanted. God can heal by changing our understandings and our emotions. When we think about it, obviously God wanted us on the earth, or we wouldn't be here!

I had built a wall around myself thinking I had to take care of everything and could not depend on others to help me. I had unconsciously decided I was only loveable if and when I can help others. This statement had become an "inner vow" for me, which in turn had a way of locking me into a hard role, behaving the very way I wanted to avoid. I learned through the Mirror Images program that I had to take off my mask of competence and learn to state my emotional needs and become willing to ask for help. I did not need to be or feel alone emotionally. I learned I could trust others with even my negative emotions, which I had always judged and hidden as weakness.

To receive nurturing I had to admit I needed nurturing. I had been giving people the impression I was someone who had no needs, not who I really was. My husband Terry says, "Pride is telling people who you are NOT."

My decision, at the age of ten, to care for myself seemed like the most logical thing for me to do, at that time, as a result of my observations of my mom and dad's struggles with each other, and my siblings. My plan for my life had been to cause as little trouble as possible and always "be the helper." I needed to learn to focus on my own feelings more and let others make their own choices and maybe even fail if they were going to learn anything from their life experiences.

Believing and acting as if our perceptions and purposes are the best for others, does not give others a chance to interpret or live life for themselves. Our children or others do not have the opportunity to make their own choices, to accept the challenges and learn from their own understanding. Maturation comes as an individual begins to make their own life choices, to live with the consequences of those choices, and learn from these consequences.

MASKS AND GAMES WE PLAY

As honest adults we can face the reality that we have worn false faces or masks pretending to be and do what others expect of us. My mask is generated by my expectations of what they want from me. We play the games we think are directed by others rather than fulfilling our own innate directives or desires. We do not do what we want to do, but what we think others want us to do. We have done what others expect, to gain their attention and approval.

We may have continuously denied our own feelings and special gifts (Romans 12: 6-8) to gain the acceptance we want and need from those around us, always trying to please them. As we step back, we can see false images we have presented to others and the games we have played with them.

When we honestly examine these situations, especially those times when we find we are resentful of what we are doing, we need to examine the situation. We must learn to speak the truth about our own feelings and expectations to become authentic individuals. When we become authentic and speak the truth, we can order our behavior and energies in a way that we can accomplish much of what was intended for us. When we walk in our motivational gifts (Romans 12) we can do so with joy and a sense of fulfillment.

When we are through playing the games we thought were required of us to make a relationship work, our energies can be redirected. We can stop trying to read others' expectations and stop placing our expectations on them. The individual who has always been compliant in attempts to please others by honoring their expectations will begin to recognize their own needs and begin to say "no" to the requests of others. This will be shocking to those who have always been using our willing service to fulfill their expectations. A visible expression of surprise from others may accompany the new negative response from the usually over-compliant "yes" player. Our responses should be, as directed scripturally, "Our yes means yes, and our no means no." (James 5.12)

Angry outbursts can be masks of uncertainty. The angry mask helps to push others away from a situation when the individual may not know how to react appropriately.

Resentment can be recognized as a mask of compliance. Resentment is a key to inappropriate servitude behavior. God has called us as servants to all, but he also has definite plans for us which may become muddled with our overzealous compliance to another's direction rather than His, internally recognized by self. Capable people often find themselves overcommitted to helping others to the extent that their lives become overburdened or over scheduled. Seeking to please others can become a mask of compliance when actually the person finds their own plans curtailed and they have bent to do another's directives.

Masks cover the person's authentic and true, appropriate feelings and attitudes. Each person should come to a place of being willing to express their own desires, attitudes and plans within each and every relationship with honor and respect for themselves and the others involved. Compromise, rescheduling, accommodation and companionship should all be a part of any mature relationship.

187

It was very hard for me not to be jealous of those who appear to have close family ties. What I need to accept is that God's plan for me and my family is entirely different from any other. I cannot compare my life to others. It is a real danger and recipe for resentment to look over the fence at others' lives, when I don't know the whole story. I have learned to be grateful for what is going well in my own life.

I attended a family birthday party for my sister-in-law Betty. I called Betty later to say how touched I was as I observed her father's loving care of his wife, Betty's senile mother. Betty's dad told me it was "his joy" to care for his ailing wife. His response brought me to tears. I shared this story with my sister-in-law Betty and she laughed saying, "That was remarkable he said that, considering how self-centered and selfish he had been his whole life!"

She added that she was so surprised her girls had given her the surprise party, saying this was so out of character for them to do such a thing! There I was staring my "idealistic" thinking in the face, and I had to laugh at myself. That took care of my "illusions" of their perfect family! Lord, heal me of this and give me a grateful heart for what I do have! God loves hearts that are content.

Throughout our family struggles, one dilemma after another, I decided I must keep on learning more about myself, my relationships, and my communication skills. I have been open to classes, workshops and other groups knowing as I learn from others I can pass on what I learn to other hurting people.

I walked into an introductory class on mental health issues, expecting to be one of five or six people, but the room was filled with thirty-eight people. Each person had their own story of pain and heartache, as we watched loved ones struggle with life. As we went around the room and heard each person's concerns, I thanked God for directing me to this place. Finally, there were some people who knew how I felt, who struggled with the same types of issues with adult children. At this meeting, I realized our family has more mental health disabilities than I had considered previously.

God never intended for parents to carry adult children's problems. Father God was calling me to trust Him more. I had to learn to love myself enough to say, "The relationship of child and mother is two-way. I cannot maintain it by myself. If it is broken it is my child's loss as well. I am a nice person and I can be OK and enjoy life, whether my child wants to be a part of my life or not."

Terry and I attended a weeklong Mirror Images Retreat program founded by Dr. Sonja Kvale. This program helped me to reconcile more with my son Chad. I wrote to Chad, sharing my wounds about the distance in our relationship. He responded with a long letter that also gave me some insight into his heart. At least we are moving toward a more authentic relationship.

Our relationships with our siblings from our families of origin have also changed as we willingly share our own hurts and damages of our childhoods. Our actions have opened the communication within our family members to a new place of transparency and trust.

Our job as parents is to love our adult children, pray for them, and encourage them whenever we can. We've had to set some very firm boundaries with our children because of their attempts to get their own way in certain situations. We learned a phrase in counseling about being *respectful of our children's chaos* and letting them own their own struggles. They have often invited us into their chaos, but we had to learn to say, "No thanks, we trust you to work this out."

This posture has worked well for us and we have watched our adult children make some very mature decisions. We have also watched them make some dangerously impulsive decisions. As we pray, and let them handle their affairs, we see they have unexpected strength. They are learning as they make their own choices and live with the consequences. What a joy it is to see us move into adult relationships with our children. God has shown Himself faithful to "watch over" us.

> "Yet I am not ashamed, because I know whom I have believed, and am convinced that He is able to guard what I have entrusted to Him, for that day." 2 Timothy 1:12

29

Update on Our Family

God has tremendously blessed Terry and me with our family.

I am grateful our family members are alive, because where there is life, there is hope. I know of many biological families with brokenness, bitterness, and unforgiveness. I have finally come to terms with the fact that few people, if any, have the "perfect" family! Our pastor once said, "We are all *just one person* away from dysfunction in all our relationships."

I have learned to take responsibility for only my part in family communications, and realize that I am accountable only for my part. We all love each other and I am grateful for that. Some of our family members don't like each other, and that is their personal issue to settle, not mine. I know this is true in biological families, also.

So where is everyone today?

Jason has a continuing friendship with his birth mother and half-sister. The amazing incident in their relationship is that they gave each other the "same" music as a Christmas gift. They were both astonished, had a lot of laughs, and saw the deep significance of their family ties. This connection seemed to validate and tickle Jason, having a blood relative so like him, even liking the same music!

When Jason's birth father died unexpectedly several years ago we attended the funeral with our son Jason. Jason walked into the service behind the casket, arm and arm down the aisle with his birth mom and half-sister. We gave our condolences to Judy, the widow, Jason's birth mom. She was gracious as she always has been to us. As we sat in the church waiting for the funeral procession to enter, I was remembering events from the last thirty-eight years with our son. I was thanking God for His goodness to us to allow us to be at this funeral, completing the circle of life for someone very important in our son's life.

Jason's mother Judy has visited his home since that time.

Jason has married for the third time. He has joint custody of his son from his second marriage and his present wife has a child the same age. Both Jason and his wife have repeatedly reported how happy they are. The relationship seems very open and accepting. Jason's wife Rene knows his entire story as Jason purposed to be honest about his past. Rene accepts his past struggles, and sees Jason for who he has become. We are hopeful this will be a permanent fulfilling relationship for both of them. Jason has worked hard in recovery to come to a place where he can enjoy intimacy. They have had two more children born to their family. We are delighted for both of them. Jason is a stay at home dad, still in twelve-step recovery, and our good friend. He continues to search for the meaning of life in many readings, through many faiths, and has been called a "mystic" by one of his friends. He attends counseling, always working towards resolution and better relationships.

We love Jason because he is our son, and trust Jason into God's care. Jason has taught us much through his recovery, and we are grateful for our mutual love.

Mandy has been riddled with health crisis over the last three years. She has had at least six heart attacks, has eleven stents in her heart and has suffered severe pancreatitis this past eighteen months. Mandy admits the pancreatitis is from alcohol abuse and that she refused to heed the warning signs. Mandy became critically ill several times to the point of facing death, but she is still alive. Her current struggle is against addiction to pain meds to curb the pain caused by the pancreas. I have repeatedly asked her to go to an inpatient treatment program.

Mandy has had a change of heart due to the near death experiences. I believe she has had a very real encounter with the Lord and does trust herself into His hands, to the best of her ability. We have prayed together, and she calls on God in her crisis times. She listens to Christian teachings on T.V. and has a greater measure of peace from hearing the truth. Mandy has come to us to ask forgiveness for some very painful decisions she made. It is amazing to me the restorative power released in a relationship when someone acknowledges their sin and asks forgiveness. Jesus' accepting death on the cross to pay the price for our sins is truly the answer to bring peace and reconciliation. Mandy has found a counselor and is beginning to face her own pain.

Tyesha and Jewel committed a felony at ages 17 and 16 respectively; this landed them in juvenile correction facilities for a year of their lives. Tyesha went on to prison for two years after committing a felony in the juvenile center. She did complete her high school diploma in prison.

Jewel responded very well to the rehabilitative program in the juvenile center. She left the program prematurely, eager to "do it on her own", which she has done, working full time, getting a G.E.D. and living in her own apartment. Jewel has struggles with male dependency and has had several abusive relationships. We keep praying she will believe she is worthy of love and being cherished.

Both are now free of any legal involvement, having paid their dues for their crime.

Tyesha was released from prison, moved home to her mom's, and Mandy invited Tyesha's boyfriend to come live with them. The couple now has a darling baby daughter, London. Tyesha and Ken are very good parents to the baby. Ken works full time, and they live a relatively peaceful life.

Mandy has responded well to being a grandmother, getting great delight watching the baby's development. She admits she missed it with the girls and enjoys London a lot.

Her husband James, who never had his own children, is a very adoring grandpa to London. It is fulfilling to see them enjoy the baby, our fifth great grandchild. She is darling and strongly resembles Tyesha as a baby. We are happy to see their family rally together and care for London.

Mandy has thanked us many times for intervening in her life and taking the girls from her for that time. She says we saved their lives. Our hope is that some of the values we taught the girls will be ones they choose for themselves. We visit each one individually, and have them all over for family holidays. My heart broke when the girls were incarcerated but in retrospect I think it was God protecting them and getting them off the streets for a time to mature, and learn some self-discipline.

Mandy spends most days on her sofa because of all her health issues. For a while we held back on making plans for our life based on Mandy's condition. After one year of watching her health go up and down I decided to go on with my life as much as I can, not waiting for something bad to happen. I try to use the SET principle with Mandy, sympathy, empathy, and truth in communicating. I learned this in the Parent to Parent Classes at Nami (National Alliance on Mental Illness). When she shares her painful episodes I give sympathy, tell her I am sad, which I truly am for her with all the physical pain, and then speak truth such as, "You need to be extremely careful and follow the

Doctors orders on what you eat and drink with such severe pancreatitis. It can't heal if you don't follow protocol."

We love Mandy for who she is, not who we want her to be. Earlier in this journey I had written that Mandy is totally unaware of all the pain she imposes on the family. She had read that draft of my manuscript and said the writing was good about her but she didn't like me saying that last part about her not comprehending the hurt she had caused. I stated she was in charge of changing that ending. I think she has some understanding of that concept now that she has almost died. God has been gracious to all of us, giving us all more time with Mandy.

As time goes on, we watch the trail of broken relationships behind our son Chad. It is painful, and we feel helpless. Chad's wife Sue divorced him and moved to another town and cares for their two children. Sue resigned herself to the fact that Chad chooses his life, so she chose to go on with hers. Leah, the mother of Chad's first child, lets us go directly through her to visit our granddaughter Tara whenever we want. Chad had a new girlfriend who is an adopted Korean. They lived together for six years. She took care of Chad both financially and emotionally. She left. He works full time and see his children regularly. Our relationship with Chad is growing closer, as we are all willing to address our part in the struggles between us with truth.

We feel grateful for any contact we have with Chad and are always grateful that we can see our grandchildren as we desire. We have continued relationships with the two mothers of Chad's children, our grandchildren. They continue to keep in regular touch with us about events in their lives and send us family pictures. We all have a common bond of wanting more relationship with Chad.

Most of our family members yearn for more time with Chad but he continues to be emotionally distant from us. One year, "Chef Chad" cooked a gourmet Thanksgiving dinner for the whole family, which delighted us all.

Jenna and her husband had two children before they filed for a divorce. She entered into another short relationship soon after the divorce. Jenna and Nate got back together, had a third child but still had an on-and-off again relationship. Sick and tired of the broken relationship, Jenna chose to attend a Mirror Images Retreat, where she faced her issues. At that time, Jenna chose to forgive and release her birth mother for keeping her two older siblings while choosing to place her for adoption. She was able to accept her Korean heritage and finally contacted her birth mother because of medical questions. Jenna has had sporadic e-mail communication with one of her birth sisters, who speaks English. Jenna learned her birth mother also raised neither of her sisters, but both were given over to the Grandmother's care. This has given her a realization that she is not the only child her mother abandoned, as she had previously understood.

Nate and Jenna have matured with the biggest change being that each partner is more willing to look at their own responsibility in the relationship, rather than blaming each other. We have also seen Nate change following a commitment to the Lord. They seem to be happier as a couple.

We are grateful Jenna made the Mirror Images Retreat and faced her abandonment issues, which has helped her let go of her anger. Jenna's physical countenance has changed; she is much softer and approachable. Jenna seems to be able to love and accept herself, making all the difference in how she relates to others. We are good friends now as well as mother and daughter. Jenna's family lives close by and we all greatly enjoy doing family activities and vacations together.

Jenna and Nate recently remarried in a touching ceremony in our home. Jenna bubbled over with ideas for all the decorating. They had about twenty close friends and relatives here. It was sweet to look around and see the support system God set in place to help their family in its journey. Their pastors prayed over the family as Nate and Jenna cried softly in each other's arms. Our God is a God of restoration! Terry and I thanked God for allowing us to be a part of their healing.

Todd graduated from the University of Hawaii with a business degree. He loves his family but lived away 8 years because he could not "stand all the drama." He has moved back, found a job and is reconsidering where life will go from here! We enjoyed the two years our son lived with us before he found his own apartment.

Todd loved living in the warm climate where his Korean heredity caused him to be accepted as a "local." He called me his first day of class in Hawaii to tell me how strange it was to look around the room and see all these people who looked just like him. He said it "threw him off" for a minute and then he laughed to himself, for still feeling "white" inside.

Todd has managed the ADD quite well and has learned that regular exercise is vital to staying emotionally balanced. He admits he's afraid of a committed relationship, for fear of being rejected (*or perhaps fear of facing the parenting issues of his siblings?*) He has been the most accepting of his Asian heritage, and jokes about it frequently.

Todd remains single saying he is too nervous to raise children; he would always be fretting about their care. How deeply the events of our family's turmoil have shaped Todd's decision God only knows. Todd is a favorite uncle to all the nieces and nephews.

At the time we adopted our Asian children, we naively had no concept of what our children would encounter living in a white environment. We know social agencies are now better at educating new families about the tension racial issues create for a child placed in a white family. Cross-cultural adoption has expanded our lives in many beautiful ways. Learning about Korean and Afro-American cultures has made us more loving, and more accepting of others. God had marvelous creativity when He created man in so many different "tribes and tongues." Now when we see an all-white baby, Terry and I think they look awfully pale compared to our beautiful olive skinned, mixed race grandchildren.

Our two foster daughters live near us. Because both their parents are deceased we became family and are close friends. We enjoy each other and share watching our families grow together. Both Krista and Katie are believers so we also have a strong spiritual connection. Katie started her healing journey when she was about 35 years old. They have been faithful prayer partners with us for our extended families. They have blessed us with six grandchildren and four great-grandchildren. We really enjoy seeing the generations go on.

Through the years we have had the profound joy of watching Krista and Katie heal from their broken hearts of losing both parents, embrace Jesus' healing power, and become awesome women of God.

God has used both ladies in many ways and in many places to pray healing for others who suffered abandonment. They have brought many times more joy to our lives than we ever gave out to them in those few years they lived with us. We consider Krista and Katie our special daughters and close friends!

Truly God has blessed me abundantly during these years since my bout with cancer. God only promises us today. We don't really know if we will have the next breath. I am a grateful grandmother loving the moments God has given me with the grandchildren.

I had the privilege of taking five of our grandchildren, ages five to nine years old to a Christmas Concert. They were eager to be with me, and eager to be together. We had second row seats, which were great for active little minds. As soon as the music started one of the five year olds started wiggling her little bottom to the beat, and she never let up through the entire concert. It was such a joy to watch their delight. I had been at this same church, almost four years earlier to the day, right before my cancer surgery. This day had been different, a totally joyous event!

Terry and I have observed that nature has a very significant role as we observe our grandchildren today. We see our adult children's behaviors displayed through their children's precious and unique mannerisms, inherited from their parents, our adults.

Mandy's grandchild looks exactly like Tyesha did at that age. Mandy's daughters love excitement just like mom. Chad's son has the same hand gestures Chad did at that age. Chad's son is gifted in math and music, just like his dad. Jason's firstborn son looked like a clone of Jason at 2 months old. Jenna's daughter was shy and reserved, just like mom as a toddler. Our son Jason's daughter looks identical to Jason's birth mother at that same age. Jason showed his child a photo of his birthmother and the child thought it was herself. Jason's birthfather loved to give people nicknames. Jason does the same. Mandy loves to wear wigs and get her nails done and her birthmother also loves wigs and getting her nails done. Mandy's birthmother enjoyed pull tabs, Mandy loves to gamble. Jenna is a great cook, her birthmother owned a restaurant! Krista is a very artistic lady. Her mother was an artist. Krista's oldest daughter has the same bubbly, fun-loving personality her mom has, always ready to be with people.

The genetic links are very obvious. We see that nature had a very significant influence on who our children were and are! It is a gift that God has allowed us to live and see these connections in the next generation.

My convent roommate and I recently returned to the convent to visit "Mother Superior," now ninety years old. She told us she has a journal of all the names of the girls who have been in the convent and that she prays for them all. I refreshed her memory of the many talks we had while I was deciding to leave the convent. I remember I was so fearful that I was disappointing my God and finally dared to ask her, "Will God still love me if I leave?"

She had responded, "Absolutely. Yes! You should go home because the Lord wants you to be happy and you do not seem very happy here."

Forty-seven years later, on a summer day in 2010, as my friend and I shared, this little nun cupped her hands to her face, giggled, and said, "Oh, the Holy Spirit is so wise. I would have told you the same thing today!"

I also reminded the nun that I had been told to leave by the side door because the others may be tempted by my decision to leave.

As we were leaving, she said, "Come, come," she insisted, "This time you must leave through the grand front entrance, with a big hug and my blessings."

We walked away. Looking back at her standing and waving good-bye at the gate was a serendipity moment of blessing for me I will treasure forever. I sent her flowers, thanking her for her time with us and for her prayers. She responded with a note: "Do you know what I did with the flowers? I took them right into the chapel and put them by the statue of Jesus." Terry and I wept when we heard this.

Throughout the years God has allowed me to journey throughout the world sharing His good news of salvation to many people of many nations (Mexico, India, Haiti, China, Russia, Nigeria, Spain, Israel, Romania, Turkey, Poland, Bangladesh, and Moldavia). Terry and I have continued our journeys with family and with other groups. These journeys have provided joy, purpose and respite for us from the journey of our family struggles. We were able to focus on the Lord's commission, "To go into all the world."

We have been privileged to support God's work in many countries. When Terry accompanied me to India a dream came true for me as God knit Terry's and my heart together on the importance of missions, and we have been able to have much joy in serving on short term teams to share the news that Jesus is alive and wants to save us from our sins. Our main focus has been caring for the needs of children and widows. We have wonderful contacts in many nations that we copartner with to bring the good news. God has put a desire to help orphans deep in our hearts. We have come to learn there are endless opportunities to help the world's many orphans.

The message from the Gospel that as you "give you will receive" has been proven to us over and over again. We are living proof that God is willing and able to use the wounded warriors to do His work here on planet earth!

Terry and I have also joined the team of individuals presenting the Mirror Images program. We have been retreat facilitators and presented the program with a weekly group in our home.

Terry and I are retired and enjoy many hobbies, travel, continue to do short term missionary work, and love visiting our kids and grandkids. When we celebrated our 40th wedding anniversary we had a three-day celebration with our children and grandchildren. All twenty-one of us stayed at a hotel together. Friday evening we all enjoyed the water park. Saturday we went on a train ride together and Sunday we ended the time together with a formal brunch and renewal of our vows.

Mandy told me her anniversary gift to us was to keep her family in a peaceful mood for the weekend, with no outbursts. She was so proud of herself for remaining calm, and not causing a scene. Her younger brother Todd told her that was "normal" behavior and she shouldn't be so proud, and they both laughed. I laughed and agreed with Todd, and was secretly happy to have a family gathering with no drama, for three whole days. It was a record for our family time together!

We thank God for our five children, 19 precious grandchildren, and six great grandchildren. The question comes up; would we do it again? Yes! Yes! Yes!

I have a dear friend who reminds me, "Josie, the last chapter isn't written yet!"

> "He settles the barren woman in her home as a happy mother of children. Praise the Lord!" Psalm 113:9

Webster defines 'settled' as, "come to rest; to set in place so as to be firmly or comfortably situated." I am definitely at rest and firmly situated in my identity as mom to five beautiful people and two foster daughters. As I said earlier, my season of feeling barren was short lived since we have had children in our hearts and home our entire life. God has been good to Josie Jones!

This book was conceived in my heart and has taken years from conception to completion! Let's say, I am glad I didn't know the future. Sonja suggested the subtitle for the book, "an adoption survival story." I was taken aback at first, thinking that was harsh. But we all have survived a lot of pain inflicted on one another, because of our own life experiences. We wanted a family. God gave us our family. Every family has issues. We have wonderful children, good memories, mixed in with some very hard painful memories. God's grace was sufficient and IS sufficient for us. The title of "Many Waters Cannot Quench Love" is a truth for Terry and me. We have had many storms and floods, but it has not dampened our love for each other, nor our love and commitment to our family. We know that in "due season we will reap if we faint not." We enjoy each day we have as it is given to us.

Thank you for reading about our journey. I am open to hear your comments about what you have learned through reading this book, and/or through your own adoption experience. You can send me an email at **josiejones07@gmail.com**.

30

Counselors Summary

Control issues are one of the major conflicts for an abandoned, adopted, and/or abused child. An adult who had been adopted reports that as a child she often felt she was unable to breathe. She now understands that these were the times she was trying to find "something or someplace" where she had some control. When she felt unable to control the person or situation, she felt she was unable to breath. The individual unconsciously attempts to find situations and relationships where they have control of something: space, relationships, and interaction. Because of the overall pervasive sense of worthlessness, they unconsciously work towards a place where they can "call the shots" and find their worth by being in control of some aspect of their life.

Repeated "escapes" from others' decisions may be seen as attempts to control their own space even by making their own choices and relationships. One adoptee stated she never wanted to be or play by herself. Another describes her lifestyle as an over-achiever as an attempt to control herself in a manner she deemed necessary. She was a compliant child in an attempt to please the authority figures in her life. Her energies were focused on safeguarding and controlling her place by proving she had great ability and worth in every way she knew.

The search for the whole truth is a healthy endeavor for each of us. Those courageous enough will dare to look at their childhood perceptions to retrieve the truth by review and reinterpretation with the additional input of others' realities to know the whole truth. Knowing that there has been a plan by a Creator God for each life (Psalm 139:11-14) may give an individual the courage to look and discover that everything may ultimately work together for the good of each person (Romans 8:28).

Someone once explained the impact of including new additional family members by using the analogy of lighting another candle for each new person within the family. One candle represents the love light between two people. When you use the light of one lit candle to light another candle it does not in any way diminish the light given off by the first candle, but two lit candles doubles the amount of light available to the whole room. Loving one person is not diminished in any way by adding another individual into a loving relationship. Loving an adoptive mother or sibling does not diminish the love for any other sibling added along the journey of life. The love or light emitted only fills the room or world around with the increasing love or light available to all present.

Whenever the issue of adoption is presented in a realistic manner such as Josie's story, the importance of presenting another example of the downside of an abortion choice is necessary. Life is hard; there are no easy choices. Relationships within a family are as difficult as those outside of the family. People need to learn and adjust to one another all throughout life and each choice has a consequence.

In Celebrate Life magazine, Nancy Kreuzer (2004) clearly described the emotional pain she has experienced since her choice of abortion, fifteen years earlier:

> *"I have new questions these days. What could I say, what could I show someone contemplating abortion? Could I tell them that the damage to their soul would require such intense healing that no one, short of the Lord, could heal the depth of that wound?*

"Could I tell them that the pain of that decision would remain hidden like a heavy weight until one day, they would have to come to terms with it, one way or another? Could they comprehend the shame that eventually seeps into one's consciousness and the shock that follows? Could they simply and blindly go forward with their lives for so many years without mention of the baby they had aborted?

"Could I paint for them a picture of experiencing that sick feeling, deep in the gut, that eventually gives rise to words that sound more animal than human and the subsequent groan, 'How could I have done this to my baby?' Could I explain to them that one day, like me they might find themselves driving along in their car or sitting quietly at home and suddenly remember sitting in the abortion facility's waiting room, vividly recalling the fluttering, low on the left side of their abdomen—the movement of their preborn child?

"I went on to have another baby who everyone called a 'perfect' baby boy. But I remember with a mother's grief, my little girl—Melanie, I named her. I never talked about Melanie to anyone. No one knew her name. The anniversary of her death would pass silently each year, and I honored her short life alone in the chambers of my heart.

"I think about how much a not so-'perfect' baby could have meant to me and to others who might have known her, had she lived. I think about the loss for the world—how she might have helped straighten out our twisted thinking—the perverse standard that defines who is good enough to keep and who we see as imperfect enough to throw away."

An unplanned pregnancy is a very challenging situation and any choice that is made will consist of pain. Josie's story shows the struggle both adopted children and adoptive parents face. The difference between Josie's story and a story that ends in abortion is love. The Jones family has ups and downs like any family on earth. But Terry and Josie were blessed with the chance to love five amazing children because five women made the difficult choice of adoption.

Addendum A: Revisiting Infertility Grief

We investigated adoption the very first week we learned we had very low probability of pregnancy. We had no hesitation to proceed. Our first child came home within four months of the time we applied.

One lovely fall day my sister in law and I were having coffee when she asked me how I had dealt with the disappointment of infertility. I told her that I guess I didn't feel I needed to since we had a family!! She said she would have been really angry with God, so she was sure glad it hadn't happened to her. After she left, I mused with the Lord, and said; "well what about this?" I heard Him say to me Jeremiah 29:11, "For I know the plans I have for you, plans to give you a future and a hope." I did have tears and sadness when I would hear of friends being pregnant who didn't even want to be! I trusted God! I never really felt empty because I was busy with two and then four children (the foster daughters) in three years' time!

Our first two children came to us easily. Abortion was not legal in our land! I actually felt relieved that I didn't have to go through all the trials of labor and delivery; there were plenty of grueling details at most baby showers. I eventually dreaded going to baby showers because it reminded me that I was different from most women.

I was blessed that my children slept through the night, usually from the first week they came home. I didn't think I had missed too much.

As I said earlier we moved to adoption easily and I didn't have deep prolonged pain about not having a pregnancy. When we had our first grandchild, Tyesha, the gravity of the generational and genetic

208

aspects of infertility really impacted my emotions. I was totally blindsided by my response at this time. Mandy and Peanut were teasing each other about who the baby looked like the most. We joined in their joy, comparing the baby's physical features with her parents. While driving home it dawned on me that I would never hear anyone say, "Oh he looks just like you!" I would not be able to identify Terry's nose or my hair with any other person. Early on I had joked that at least our kids never had to say, "Oh I have mom's big hips, or dad's large nose." But now it seemed too final. I had rationalized that at least ALL our kids were beautiful, and all of them had talents Terry and I didn't, like singing, writing, and playing the piano.

Another time when I feel deep sadness is holding a newborn grandchild and realizing I missed all those precious first days with my own children. Each day seemed so precious and babies change so quickly. That is when the grief comes to the surface again. I feel the loss of all those times to cuddle, and feed them, and bond with them early in their lives. I have reflected on many of our struggles, and mused that *if only* I had been able to be there since day one, life would be different. I am still sad that I couldn't have them since day one, because now in retrospect, I believe the first days are so valuable in settling their hearts with trust through the caregiver. My children each had several caregivers before they became ours.

My secret hope was always that even though my children would not look like me physically, that they would emulate our spiritual beliefs. This has happened with our foster daughters, and several of our children. I have had to let go of many expectations on my children, and let them each find their unique way, and spiritual path in life.

My niece, taking fertility drugs as we had done, shared her grief and the tension they experienced while waiting every month to see if she was pregnant. We also talked about the sadness we felt seeing others getting pregnant so easily. Later that night the Lord spoke to me and said, "You don't know what I protected you from!" That thought really surprised me. I reflected back, "Yes Lord You are Sovereign and know the beginning from the end."

When I was fifty-three someone told me you could get pregnant in menopause, and should consider using birth control, so I discussed this with Terry. He was so sweet, gentle, and funny, as usual. He laughed at the idea.

I continued asking, "But what if I did show up pregnant, now that we're old?"

Terry beamed with a big smile, "I'd be proud as a peacock!"

That tickled me a lot, and relieved any doubts I had. He has never seemed to care, nor has he said one word about feeling less of himself, or about us as a couple or the fact that our family was not biological.

I decided that it doesn't matter if someone has my hips or Terry's nose or laugh. What matters is that I love my family, that they are nurtured and that we introduced them to the Author of Love, Jesus Christ. It is more important to build character, faith, hope, and joy in their lives than to pass on our physical features.

Addendum B: Family Mental Health Issues

My first assignment as a social worker for the county was to serve patients at the state hospital for the mentally ill. In the 60's people were court ordered to the hospital for various lengths of time and sometimes for life. They lived in Spartan conditions, with little to no therapy, often heavily medicated to keep them calm. My heart broke for the people I saw there. Some improved and left the hospital after several months stay and returned to their families.

Mental health is not easily defined. My definition of mental health is having stability in our thinking, knowing realistically who we are, and relating with other people in a give and take fashion, where there is benefit for both parties in the relationship. Mental health issues often occur when a person's thinking gets stuck in one thought process. They can be so self-focused or self-absorbed, that all relationships are filtered through their grid of delusion or illusion. People are said to have "mental problems" when their emotions are frequently out of control. One definition of "crazy" is repeating the same thing, hoping to get different results. A definition given to us in the Parent to Parent Class at National Association on Mental Health was "people are mentally ill when they are not able to empathize with others".

After becoming a born again Christian in 1979 and learning about Jesus' healing powers I had a great zeal to have those who struggle be "delivered" from their mental sickness. I had faith and hope that the problem was spiritual and prayer was the answer. For forty years I have repeatedly asked the Lord for clarity about mental health issues, yet today I have no clear answers.

I have witnessed people who suffered with mental health issues become believers, pray, study the Word, and renew their minds, and I have seen them improve. I have prayed with people for deliverance from spirits that I believe harassed them. I have seen these people improve also; but only when they continue to guard their thought lives and fill their minds with good things. I have seen Christians who love God, pray and read their Bibles regularly, take their meds from the Doctor conscientiously, and still struggle with times of mental instability.

I think most of us know a recovering alcoholic or drug addict. Their behavior was "crazy" while they used. We may even have labeled them mentally ill. But as they embraced sobriety they began to act more "normal", make right decisions and live their lives more connected to people, admitting they were wrong, and asking for forgiveness. They began to own their own mistakes. They began to admit their own powerlessness, to admit that a power greater than them was at work, and they began to enjoy life more. Their behavior changed as their thinking changed.

When a person's thinking (mental state) is unstable, irrational, depressed, how do I respond? Do I say it's a chemical imbalance in their body and give them medicine, do I pray for them, or do I counsel them to talk and get the emotions out and dealt with? I think all three are appropriate methods to bring someone to "mental'" health and peace and stability.

Is it genetic imbalances, sin or a character defect that cause someone so much trouble in relationships? Only God really knows. He made each of us. He knows us intimately. We are called to be His children, to walk in His nature. As I told you I was adopted into God's family. I don't have his nature. It is my call to become Christ-like by changing my thinking about myself and life; to become all He intended me to be. His nature starts operating in me as I yield my thought life over to Him. Perhaps the bad behavior is just plain selfishness, anger, hurt, fear, or rage on my part. Are these just character flaws, my genetic disposition, or am I accountable to improve my responses in order to have peaceful relationships?

I have learned there is a spiritual dimension in effect in the world, God's kingdom of light, and the devil's kingdom of darkness, pulling at us. We get to decide which kingdom or spirit realm we want to walk in, think in, and believe in. The devil tries to fill our minds with thoughts or lies to discourage us. The Bible speaks of God's great love for us and how He thinks of us and what He has done for us.

The devil has come to "steal rob and destroy." John 10:10. The devil tried to get Jesus to believe the lies he spoke to Jesus. I, Josie, need to refute the lies he tries to whisper to me; "Mandy will never change! You're a terrible mom; you failed miserably! You don't deserve to be forgiven for some of the choices you made as a parent!" I need to attack these thoughts with the truth:

1) Things may not change but I can still be happy and content in the Lord.

2) Yes I did make mistakes, and I can forgive myself, I can ask forgiveness of those I hurt, and take responsibility and move on.

3) I get to make choices each day that lead to a better life.

Sonja has been a mental health professional for over 20 years. She dislikes "labels" placed on people defining a person as "an illness," be it depressed, bi-polar, narcissistic, etc. I see labels or "Diagnosis" as a way to try to understand what is happening with a person. It helps me have a place to put all the erratic behavior. The person with the diagnosis is still someone's mom, sister, son, daughter, and friend. We must love them, listen to them, and communicate truth to them.

Did my sister Tess act mentally ill when she started the fires? Yes. Did she have great reason to be confused and raging? Yes. Did shock treatment help her cope? Yes, to a degree. Did forgiving her perpetrators help her? Yes. Did meds help her sleep? Yes. Many of her problems were directly related to the sexual abuse from our brothers. It was no accident she set fire to the perpetrators' mattresses and then our parents' mattress. She had told my mom and mom didn't believe her. My sister Tess, in her late twenties, had thirty shock treatments in an attempt to cure her depression. At age 55 Tess became a Christian and has been renewing her mind with the truth of God's Word, forgiving her perpetrators and walking in a greater measure of peace than ever before. She is still on medicine.

There are three people in the Bible who suffered from mental illness. King Saul enjoyed David's music some days yet tried to kill him on other days over a thirteen year period (1 Samuel 16:14-23). Nebuchadnezzar, King of Babylon, fell from his throne and ate grass for seven years (Daniel 4:28-34). He was restored to his kingdom when he repented and acknowledged God. The Gerazene demoniac is in the story where Jesus casts many demons into a herd of pigs and the man regained his mind (Mark 5: 1-20). I know God is Sovereign and he can heal whomever He wants to whenever He wants to. Let's not judge why someone's mind is not tracking correctly. Let's speak the truth in love to them, using the medical professionals for the relief they can offer (eg. lithium for Bi-polar, or Zoloft for depression). Let's keep praying for people. Encourage them to release the pain they carry in their hearts. As they embrace truth they will find freedom.

The debate of nature versus nurture is one we have lived for 41 years. Our children are a product of our nurturing and their biological parents' DNA. Which prevails? Both are significant in shaping who they are today. My parents at the point of conception gave my own genetic package to me. I develop my character throughout my life, and my interpretation of what is happening around me. I am accountable to keep my relationships as healthy as I can, using all the tools Father God has provided for me.

Whether I think it is a mental health problem, a sin problem, or a physical problem I need to respond in a truthful, respectful, and loving manner. I can choose to walk away and end the relationship. I have to decide what boundaries I will have in the relationship to feel safe myself and honor the other person. This can be very challenging when you love someone but the relationship is toxic. The Holy Spirit is always waiting to help us find a peaceful resolution using all the fields of expertise available.

Mental Health care professionals, whether counselors, psychologists, or psychiatrists, are required to evaluate an individual in terms of their behavioral disorders or problems. The diagnostic manual used for insurance purposes has a listing of symptomatic behaviors and their variations. These numerical codes are used along with additional numbers, which indicate an evaluation of the intensity of these disorders in regard to how their behavior is damaging their relationships. Professionals use this numerical code as a "diagnosis label" for the behavioral problems, for prescribing appropriate meds and granting insurance coverage.

I have concerns about these labels. Often family, and perhaps even the professionals involved, will accept the identifying behaviors as "normal" for such-and-such a diagnosis and subsequently lower their expectations of acceptable behavior from these individuals. If the relationships of this individual are being stretched and destroyed by the behaviors, appropriate treatment should attempt to change the behaviors. Reassessments should be done periodically.

The most effective treatment for the diagnosis of "depression" is known to be the combination of therapy coupled with prescription antidepressant medications. If the medications are helpful they can be continued. My experience has been when the depression is an emotional depression due to life situations of loss and grief the medications will eventually create an abnormal fog or numbing for the individual and should be decreased and eliminated at that point. Our culture has gotten to a place of thinking that sadness and tears are not appropriate behavior; however, this is not valid. There are times in our lives when sadness and tears are the only natural reaction to life: death of a loved one, broken relationships, etc. Commercials on television peddle antidepressants as self-prescribed for the hard times of life. The walk-in patient informing their own physicians prescribing their own mental health medications is not appropriate, but the practice has become financially motivating for doctors. When we are sad, we should weep. Tears were a gift for us to help us express feelings when we have no words for the expression of these deep feelings.

People with extreme personality disorders that are destructive to the people in their lives should be brought to the attention of mental health professionals. Family members need to seek help from those understanding these situations so that they can appropriately relate to the individuals with the disorders. They need to find out if and when medications may help to diminish the behaviors, and when and how to establish appropriate guidelines for their relationships.

Josie is right in her understanding that such behaviors may be physical, emotional or even spiritual. A physically based condition, such as clinical depression, can be regulated with the appropriate medications. There are unending variations and combinations of psychotropic medications which may be beneficial to someone who has a physical basis for their behavior disorders. Physically based disorders may mean a lifetime of monitoring medications.

The treatment for the mental disorders, medication together with talk therapy, should help the individual make significant changes in their behavior assisting them to live in more satisfactory relationships with the people in their lives. If the treatment is refused or not satisfactory, there may be a time when the family must walk away so that the family unit itself is not destroyed.

Behavioral choices involving destructive behaviors, such as addictions, require awareness of damages to the relationships involved, which should be followed by a personal determination of the addicted person to seek help stopping the addiction.

Reenactment of past failure often occurs for individuals who keep living without realization or understanding of the destruction that has occurred in their own lives. Often denial and continued behavior may be an unconscious attempt to understand the events of their lives that have been damaging for them during their developmental years. An example of reenactment in the lives of adopted children is that they may find themselves inadvertently in a place of needing to decide whether or not they should give their own children up for adoption or foster care in an unconscious attempt to understand how their own parents could have given them away. Hard family situations (divorce, separation, and/or felonies, etc.) involving parents may unconsciously direct the behavior of the children as they mature, in an attempt to understand their parents.

Spiritually based behavior problems can be dealt with spiritually. Spiritual discernment is required for these situations. There are sexual disorders that have a spiritual basis. Most spiritually rooted disorders can be cast out by the continued connection with Jesus Christ and His name. For in the name of Jesus, demons have to flee (Mark 16:17).

Tragic situations result from individuals who decide that all mental or behavioral disorders are from the same source.

Mental/behavioral disorders can be based on physical, emotional and/or have spiritual roots.

And I repeat: a diagnosis of a mental disorder should not permit destructive behavior from any individual. The destructive behavior should be only an unspoken cry for help! If the individual chooses not to seek or take help, those around them must learn to set their own protective boundaries to enable them to live their lives in a place of sanity. Each of us must choose to know and understand ourselves. An individual who is willing to seek professional therapy or counsel is "half way through" because they are willing to acknowledge they need help understanding themselves.

Addendum C: Recommended Sources of Information

Beske, Beverly, Kvale, Sonja Dr.; Journey, Finding the Treasure of Family; (Story of extensive search for birth parents and siblings.)

Burland, Dr. Joyce, Family to Family Education;

NAMI 2001 (National Association on Mental Illness)

Carnes, Patrick J., PhD, Delonico, Dr. David L., Griffin, Elizabeth, MA, Mariarity, Joseph M.; In the Shadow of the Net-Breaking Free of Compulsive Online Sexual Behavior, 2001; www.amazon.com

Carnes, Dr. Patrick J.; Out of the Shadows- Understanding Sexual Addiction, 2007; www.amazon.com.

Carnes, Dr. Patrick J.; Recovery Zone Vol.I; 2009. www.amazon.com

Dorow, Sar; Editor; I Wish for You a Beautiful Life (Letters from Korean Birth Mothers); Yeong and Yeong Book So., 1999.

Elridge, Sherrie; Twenty Things Adoptive Kids Wish Their Parents Knew; Bantam Dell; a division of Random House Inc. 1999

Friesen, Dr. James, E.; The Life Model / Living from the Heart Jesus Gave You; Shepherds House Inc., Pasadena, Ca. 1999

Hall, Laurie, Affair of the Mind; (Spousal support for SA) www.amazon.com.

Hotchliss, Sandy; Why is it Always About You, Free Press, Division of Simon Schuster, Inc., 2002. (Living with Narcissism.)

Hemfelt, Dr.R; Minirith, Dr.P., Meier, Dr.F.; Love is a Choice; Thomas Nelson Publishers. 1989

Karp, David A.; The Burden of Sympathy; Oxford University Press U.S.A. 2001

Lehman, Kevin; The New Birth Order Book; Fleming Revell, 1999.

Manning, Brennan; Ruthless Trust; Harper Collins Publishers Inc. 2002

Torrey MD, E. Fuller; Surviving Schizophrenia, A Family Manual; Harper Collins Publishers. 1983

Verrier, Nancy Newton; Primal Wound, Gateway Press Inc. 2003

Wolfe, Jana; Secret thoughts of an Adoptive Mother, Andrews McNeel Publishing; 1997.

Internet Information

Carnes, Dr. Patrick J.; pinegrovetreatment.com\patrick-carnes

Delmonico, sex screening; Google

Elijah House Ministries Prayer Counseling; elijahhouse.org

Laaser, Dr. Mark, Debbie LAMFT: faithfulandtrueministries.com

Kvale, Dr. Sonja LPC; mirrorimagesretreats.org

Weiss; sexAddict.com

References

Alcoholics Anonymous 3rd Edition (1976). New York City: Alcoholics Anonymous World Services Inc.

Brandt, K (2009). *Sex Addiction: Facts and Fallacies.* Voices.yahoo.com

Fuller-Thomson, E., Minkler, M., & Driver, D. (1996). A Profile of Grandparents Raising Grandchildren in the United States. *The Gerentologist.* 37, 3.

The Holy Bible, New International Version (2002). Grand Rapids: Zondervan.

Kreuzer, N. (2009). Honest questions, Haunting Answers. *Celebrate Life.* May-June 2009, 35-36.

Leman, K. (1999). *The New Birth Order Book.* Grand Rapids: Revell.

Manning, B (2002). *Ruthless Trust.* New York: Harper Collins Publishers Inc.

Sanford, P (2009). *Healing Victims of Sexual Abuse.* Lake Mary: Charisma House.

Webster's New World Dictionary, College Edition (1957). Cleveland and New York: The World Publishing Company.